A Path Between Two Mothers

Glen Pearson

Copyright 2011 by Glen Pearson. The book author retains sole copyright to his contributions to this book.

Glen Pearson

A PATH BETWEEN TWO MOTHERS

Glen Pearson has been co-director of the London Food Bank for 25 years and spent 29 years in his career as a professional firefighter. He is also executive director of the African NGO, Canadian Aid for Southern Sudan (CASS). His ongoing community involvement and his four and a half years as a Member of Parliament and Critic for International Cooperation form the basis for the experiences found in this book. A father of seven, including three adopted children from Sudan, and grandfather of three, Pearson lives in London, Ontario with his wife Jane Roy and continues to write on the need for a more collaborative understanding of Africa and its people.

Pearson can be reached through his website

www.glenpearson.ca

TABLE OF CONTENTS

Foreword   7

Difficult Years   /   11

When Hope Ended   /   15

Moving On   /   20

Mana   /   24

I Was Always Here   /   28

Back to the Village   /   33

A Special Journey   /   42

The Package   /   47

The Conversation   /   53

Two Futures   /   59

Difficult Decisions   /   64

The Moment of Truth   /   69

Hope Fading   /   74

From Afar   /   80

Planning the Future   /   85

A Community Gathers   /   90

Taking Wing   /   95

Epilogue   /   99

FOREWORD

George Kimble once wrote, "The darkest thing about Africa has always been our ignorance of it." For almost 300 years most of us in the West have viewed it as some kind of mission station, a cause for which our assistance is required, or a people for which our more refined ways might be helpful.

For those have traveled frequently to that remarkable continent, none of the above applies. It is a place so remarkable in its beauty, suffering, complexity, and the absolute resilience of its people, that no one who has been truly touched by it can ever think the same again. Humanity was first conceived in Africa and we will return to it relentlessly until we have finally come to terms with its reality.

Originally written in 2005, *A Path Between Two Mothers* is about that one true resource that Africa possesses which is its greatest resource and legacy to the world - its people. We have heard of corruption and wars, but over 90% of the continent is too busy struggling to survive to take much notice. But in that survival lie moments of great heroism, family loyalty, community celebration, religious faith, and deep love of country.

This is a story that is largely true. Abuk has been written in as older so that her experiences of sojourn in war-ridden Sudan could be expanded. In reality, she was 13 months old when my wife Jane and I found her in a village - 15 months old when she finally came to Canada. But it took us almost one year to find her - one of the most emotional and precarious journeys of our lives.

People like the chief, commissioner, and Father Thomas are all real people, but Aben is actually a composite of three remarkable Sudanese women. Upon her mother's death she was put in the care of two sisters, who watched over her until we arrived. She lives today because of their commitment to her survival. The third women is actually named Aben and lives in London, Ontario. A deep patriot of south Sudan, whose height is as imposing as her love for her country. When Abuk first came to Canada, it was Aben and her children that assisted in the transition.

We have heard two recounts of the death of Abuk's mother. The dash for freedom from slavery actually happened, but we heard she was either killed by a landmine or was shot while holding Abuk while journeying through a minefield. We will never know exactly how she perished, but even in her death she preserved her child.

You will note references to faith often throughout the book. It is because the people of that region of south Sudan are deeply religious, having depended on their faith during the worst years of Africa's longest running civil war. In reality, the conflict itself forms one of the great overriding characters in the pages that follow - always stalking, always taking, but never overcoming.

In many ways this book is not complete. We were only to discover later that Abuk did indeed have a twin sister and a brother - two wonderful children we found totally by accident when we took Abuk back to her village five years later. Peace had come to Sudan and slavery had been ended. As a result, the two children returned from captivity along with their grandmother and just happened to be in the village on the day we arrived. It was a shock that was to change our lives. DNA testing was done and the family bond was verified.

Today these three children - Abuk (11), Achan (11), and their brother Ater (14), lived in London, Ontario where they thrive and grow relentlessly taller. Every night we gather as a family to remember the bravery and sad loss of their mother. At times it is emotional, at other times it's just sad. But what must she think if she sees them in this present state - healthy, educated, lovely, and above all, together? They live not because she died, but because she prevailed - breaking for freedom, which is the essence of human growth. Today her children stand as a testimony to that one day when she made that move for liberty. Her children are not only free and safe, they represent the best that resided in her.

And what to say of Jane? Her remarkable exploits in finding and rescuing Abuk will remain one of the greatest adventures I will ever know. I had a ringside seat, watching as destiny brought together a dying child and a new mother full of life. I recall the very moment we first spotted Abuk in her tukul as the war raged around us. She was sickly and perishing, but still Jane moved immediately to her on that cot and embraced. From that moment *A Path Between Two Mothers* had to be written as a tribute to women of great valour and to a people of Africa for whom adaptation and courage have become a common birthright. Our world is better for their presence in it and it will be eventually cured once we learn to take small strides in their remarkable footsteps.

Achan, Ater and Abuk

Difficult Years

The sun rose as it always did in this part of Sudan—shimmering and hot.

Abuk felt the heat even before she opened her eyes. The mud walls of her tukul, a Sudanese hut, kept the temperature somewhat cool and so she hesitated to get up and face the heat of the morning.

She had just awoken from the same dream she had every night and felt the sadness that always came from it. And it always ended the same, with her mother dead on the ground and Abuk crying out to no one in particular.

Things seemed so hopeful just a second before the thundering noise erupted and changed her world. Abuk's mother had been from Yargot, in south Sudan, until the day some raiders came to her village and burned it to the ground. The mother's family had been killed and she, along with a number of other young women from the village, had her hands tied and was led with the others to parts of the country she had never seen before.

The terrible things her mother had to endure remained mostly unknown to Abuk because she hadn't been born yet. But whatever they were, her mother remained strong and determined that one day she would return to her home in the south.

In language Abuk came to understand all too clearly, her mother had a "master." After being taken into captivity, her mother had been sold to a man who purchased her in a market. Now she was the property of someone else. She was "owned" by someone. This was something Abuk could never understand … or accept.

And as the property of the man, the mother had to accept some terrible things. Sometimes he was nice to her, but mostly he forced her to do things that made her angry and ashamed.

Then one day, after being a slave for almost two years, the mother discovered she was going to have a baby. From that moment she decided she would do everything she could to get back home and give her baby the chance to live a life with its own people.

Yet as hard as she tried, she never succeeded. One time she tried to sneak away in the night and almost made it into the next county. Suddenly some dogs began to bark and a group of men burst out of a tukul, recognized her and took her back to her master. He was so angry that he pushed and beat her. When he was finished, however, he was surprised to see a look of determination in the woman's eyes.

Then all thoughts of escape disappeared as the mother came close to the time of her child's birth. Her master had suddenly lost all interest in her and left her alone for a number of days.

When the right moment came, the mother asked a number of friends to her tukul and within a few hours, despite her bruises and pain, they assisted the mother in delivering a tiny baby daughter—Abuk.

For the next few years, mother and daughter, continued to live in a strange place as slaves. From her earliest memories, Abuk could recall her mother struggling and working hard to provide food and shelter for the two of them. On some days the master would provide some extra grain or fish, but mostly they were given too little food.

Since her earlier attempted escape, the master had moved Abuk's mother to a place that was more closely watched and she began to despair that she would ever see her home again. Abuk came to understand that life as a slave was perhaps the most difficult life of all because you couldn't make any decisions for yourself.

Abuk's most difficult moments didn't come from hunger or pain, however. There were certain nights when the master came to visit Abuk's mother and after he left she could hear her mother sobbing. In those times, Abuk would creep to her mother's side and slowly wiggle her way inside the woman's arms. Somehow she understood that what her mother was experiencing was something terrible and was somehow related to slavery.

Abuk's life stayed much like this until one hot summer day when she was six years old. It was a day she would never forget.

The master was growing more and more angry with Abuk's mother and when he was visited by someone who offered to pay for her and take her away, the master surprised everyone by agreeing.

Two days later, mother and daughter said goodbye to the only place Abuk had ever lived. At first Abuk felt sad as she watched the tukul fade off into the distance, but as she looked into the eyes of her mother she saw a sense of relief. And from that moment on both mother and daughter thanked God together for a chance to leave that terrible situation.

The man who had purchased them led them away, but rather than going farther north, his direction took them further south, towards the direction of the mother's home. Thinking she would still be in slavery, the mother was nevertheless comforted in knowing she would at least be closer to her home village.

Both of them waited for the new master to speak to them, but instead he would merely provide them rice and cornmeal. One time he even returned from a nearby market with a pair of plastic shoes for Abuk's mother. She didn't know what to think of it because she had never been treated like this before.

Then one night they gathered under a tree with a group of other slave women and their children. Recognizing one of them, Abuk's mother asked what was happening.

"Have you not heard?" the woman asked. "Some people from Canada have paid this man to take us to our freedom, to our homes."

Could it be? Was God this good? She pulled Abuk to her and wrapped her in her arms. The daughter put both her hands on her mother's face and attempted to wipe away the tears.

"What is it, Mana?" she whispered.

For minutes her mother could say nothing as her eyes gazed towards the south.

"Abuk, listen to me very closely," she said. "Remember all those times we asked God to bring us home, to my family and friends?"

"Yes, Mana," Abuk replied.

"Perhaps God has not forgotten us after all," her mother continued. "All this time I thought that our lives only mattered to a few people. But could it be that people from even faraway countries have prayed for us as well, asking God to bring us to freedom."

They didn't know the answer to this, of course, but that night Abuk nestled in the arms of her mother, gazing at the stars, as they both sang the same songs that had given them so much comfort over the last six years. In the familiar words they found hope.

When Hope Ended

She knew it was time to get up, but somehow the memories of singing songs with her mother filled her with a deep sadness. But it was getting too hot in the tukul and she knew she was already late for her morning chore of finding water.

She had promised Aben she would search for water every morning but at times like now, with little rain, it was difficult. And, yet, how could she refuse Aben, after all she had done?

Now as she grabbed the old plastic jug and made her way to the well that was usually dried up, her thoughts returned to her dream and once again the vision of her mother's face filled her mind.

They had sung long into the night before finally falling asleep. And in the morning when they awoke it was to a new sense of purpose. The other women were experiencing it, too. The man who was helping them was an Arab named Nadhir. Abuk discovered later that he had been secretly working with people from around the world who had worked together in an attempt to help her people get out of slavery. But it hadn't been without risk. Many of the slave masters had been looking for him when they discovered he was taking their slaves away from them.

They departed very early in the morning just before sunrise and the farther south they travelled the more Abuk noticed the landscape becoming greener in colour. In the same way she saw in her mother more and more signs of excitement that Abuk hadn't seen there before.

By evening they had traveled almost thirty kilometers and were approaching the border between north and south Sudan. Now everyone had to be very careful in case someone spotted them and reported them to the authorities.

Remaining unseen wasn't easy, but as the plants grew greener and more trees appeared, the group of women led by Nadhir managed to keep as well-hidden as possible.

At the camp that night the women wanted to start a fire, but Nadhir reminded them they could easily be spotted in the dark. The group ate some ground nuts and some water lilies they had picked earlier in the day. They were tired yet excited at the same time and many stayed up late talking about their home villages and hoping they would be there soon.

As Abuk looked at her mother, she saw she was almost asleep. Quietly, almost in a whisper, she sang

> *Beeti mama abe ben emen.*
> *man abuk abe ben emen.*
> *ye heen bi abuk ya nyan diet*
> *be man kucny n luci.*
> *be man kucny ne that.*

It was the first song her mother had taught her and now the daughter sang with pride as she realized all her mother had endured for her. Soon enough, her mother's eyes closed and Abuk fell asleep soon after.

Early the next morning a delightful but brief rain shower changed the dried ground into mud for a few hours. The women and the children looked up into the skies, letting the raindrops run down their faces. Abuk watched another child stick her tongue out and catch the droplets and she did the same. It was a new sensation for her and it caused her mother to laugh loudly at the sight.

By mid-afternoon they came across a railway line. "This is the line that leads to my village … our village," her mother said happily.

Abuk looked at the two sets of iron rails that ran perfectly straight to the southern horizon. The group never strayed more than a few meters from the rail line at any one point, almost as if it was a cord that tied them to their home.

It was while they were resting under the shade of a tree that they heard the strange sound—*whump, whump, whump*. Nadhir understood the danger immediately and called to the women wandering and gathering ground nuts to quickly hide under the trees.

But it was too late. From over the trees came something Abuk had never seen before but which resembled a large bird whose wings didn't move. Like an angry bee it swooped overhead as soon as it saw some of the women. Abuk's mother swiftly picked her up and raced with other mothers and their children down the rail line.

From over her mother's shoulder Abuk watched something she would never forget as long as she lived. The iron bird suddenly spat fire and the ground shot up dirt and mud. She saw some of the women fall to the ground and she wondered why they weren't getting up.

As the iron bird moved towards the group Abuk was in, the women instinctively tried to run for a swamp they could see nearby. And then, suddenly, some of them were screaming as different kinds of explosions came out of the ground. Abuk's mother saw a child lying on the ground behind her, ran back, grabbing the girl's hand and moved once again toward the swamp.

Abuk was just about to whisper in her mother's ear that her back was hurting because her grip was too tight when all of a sudden she heard the loudest bang she would ever hear.

It was only later that Abuk was to learn that in her hurry to find a safe place for her daughter, the mother had stepped on a landmine as she ran. Her body had kept Abuk safe as the explosion occurred.

Abuk landed hard on the ground, hurt by the sudden fall. She turned to look for her mother as the iron bird flew away in the distance.

She saw her mother lying on her back, her eyes closed, and Abuk understood immediately that she had died. As some of the other mothers and children lay close by, moaning because of their injuries, Abuk crawled to her mother's side and cried until she fell asleep.

Exactly how long she laid in the minefield no one could be sure, but some observers said it had been at least half a day. Abuk became increasingly aware of her own danger. Were there other mines close by? How many were there? Should she try to get up and run or should she stay still?

Suddenly without her mother, Abuk grew very afraid. While still holding her mother's hand she cried out for anyone to listen. From behind some trees an elderly man came out and motioned to her to be very still. He asked her if she was hurt but she just shook her head as though she didn't understand.

And then the man did something very brave. Leaning on his cane, he gazed intently at the ground and made his way toward where she was. At one point she started to stand and run to him but he told her sternly to stay still.

Finally after some minutes he stood beside her. Abuk grabbed his arm but wouldn't let her mother's hand go. "Child, it's not good for you to be here. Take my hand and follow me very closely."

The saddest moment of her life came when Abuk released her

mother's hand and gave her a final kiss on the cheek. She wept uncontrollably, knowing that the main person in her life would no longer be there to guide her, dry her tears, or lead her through life.

Moving On

Her mother's death had been two years ago now, but having the same dream over and over again made the sadness of it new to Abuk every night. She had been six years old then and had felt all alone in the world. To her, little seemed to have changed in that time.

But was that really true? As she made her way to the village well she began to think about what had happened after she had come out of the minefield.

The old man with the cane had taken her to the tukul of the village Chief and told him of all that had happened to Abuk. As he spoke of the helicopter and of the death of Abuk's mother, the Chief began to look closely at her. She grew shy then and looked down to the ground, but in the Chief's eyes she had seen kindness and concern.

The Chief had then met with the other leaders from the area and they decided that Abuk should be given to one of the village women so that she could take care of the young child.

Abuk had been too saddened since the loss of her mother to really care or understand what was happening. Yet she lived in south Sudan and she knew how hard life was; she had witnessed similar situations to her own many times.

When the village elders finally took her to Aben's home, Abuk didn't complain or run away—she simply went inside the tukul, laid down on the dirt floor, and cried herself to sleep.

She had awoken to the sound of singing. As she began rubbing the sleep from her eyes she wondered to whom the strange voice belonged and crawled to the entrance to peek out.

Aben was bending over the fire, cooking some goat meat that the leaders had provided to help in feeding Abuk. From the entrance Abuk watched as the older woman efficiently worked the fire and cooked the meal.

Without even turning around Aben said over her shoulder, "Come, child, you must be hungry."

How had Aben known she was watching? Abuk was already learning of the wisdom and understanding of this woman who had taken her on as a responsibility. Though she was still grieving the loss of her mother, the sight and smell of the goat meat mixed with rice drew her out of the tukul and to Aben's side.

"Sit there," the older woman said firmly and for the first time Abuk got a good look at her face. Aben was tall, very tall, with broad shoulders and powerful arms. But it was her face that captivated the young girl. Her smile assisted Abuk in accepting the plate of food. Aben's eyes were clear, though like so many other people in south Sudan, they also spoke of pain and suffering.

Though only six years of age at the time, Abuk understood that this woman was now to be her protector and guardian until she was older. Abuk didn't complain because this was just the way things were done in the south. Death was common and often others would care for those who had been left behind.

And, yet, Abuk still felt the deep pain of her mother's death. Quietly she chewed on the meat while staring sadly into the fire. She felt no desire to talk to or to even look at the woman.

If this concerned Aben, she didn't show it. In fact, she was glad to have a healthy portion of goat meat. The last time she had eaten anything this good was … when? … two years ago? Yet even as she ate the food hungrily her heart went out to the girl in front of her.

Aben had lost two children of her own many years ago to famine. Her husband had died in the civil war that had been going on for too many years, but she had learned over time to overcome her sadness and get on with the task of living.

Caring for Abuk was something that wouldn't be easy. The crops had failed two years in a row and the chances of finding good drinking water were becoming more and more rare.

And yet something in the look of the little girl drew compassion out of the older woman. The sadness she saw in Abuk was obvious, but more than that she discerned a strong spirit and this attracted her to the child.

"My name is Aben," she said clearly. "I know this is a difficult time for you, Abuk, but we have to work together because I now have to look after you. There is much to do and it will be hard, but I will care for you gladly."

The little girl slowly looked up and looked evenly at the woman in a way that made Aben hold her breath briefly. Abuk finished her last mouthful of rice and wiped her mouth with her arm. Then she stood up, walked to Aben, and grabbed her plate. With a dried leaf she knelt down and began the process of cleaning the dishes.

Aben watched, fascinated. Clearly this little girl had been taught well. But there was something very sad in watching her clean the plates. Only a short while ago this child had been in the arms of her loving mother and she should now be overcome with emotion at her loss. Somehow, in some way that Aben understood all too well, the child was already moving on, preparing for a future that was going to be just as difficult as her past. Nevertheless, for one so young this was very uncommon and a deep respect began to grow in Aben for the child before her.

Abuk placed the plates back in the tukul, came out again and asked, "What else would you like me to do?"

That's how it had all started, two years ago now. In the time since, Abuk had come to care deeply about Aben. It hadn't taken them long to see that they were in many ways very much alike—determined, strong, and yet quiet.

They had traveled far from the tukul in search of food, often with no success. Now, as she lowered her pail into the hole in the ground, she knew she would have no success there either. The rains had come late this season and ended early. Only on the luckiest of days could anyone find water in this well and today wasn't one of them.

Abuk sighed and felt the exhaustion that only comes to those who have very little. Life in Sudan was hard and not getting any easier. The civil war continued not many kilometers from where she now stood. The war. It was responsible for all the pains Abuk had experienced—the loss of her mother, slavery, hunger, thirst and this life of constant struggling.

And now an empty well again. She sighed once more and faced the decision in front of her. She could go back and tell Aben that there was no water again today. Or she could journey farther to the south with some of the other women in search of drinking water.

Wearily she stood up, pulled her tattered dress around her the best she could, and journeyed south.

Mana

Dry! Everywhere she went the story was the same. And increasingly she ran into other women and girls on the same desperate journey she was. Water wells which had once been the source of life for so many communities were now scenes of despair.

As the day wore on, Abuk joined a group of women and their daughters who were visiting every well and waterhole in the area. Though it was helpful for her to have company, the sadness they all felt became almost overbearing for her.

In truth, Abuk was exhausted and malnourished. In fact she had been without solid food and abundant water for the last five months and her body felt weak and unresponsive. She thought of Aben and how she, too, must be nearing the end of her hopes.

As the day was nearing its end, the rest of her group disappeared into the trees, making their way back to their villages. Abuk watched them fade in the distance and for some reason felt no desire to journey further with them. She suddenly felt very tired.

She walked to the nearest tree and stretched herself out underneath it, her eyes gazing up into its branches. This was a moment unlike any other she had experienced. It was almost like she didn't care about anything anymore. Abuk felt no desire to get up and travel back to her village before it got too dark.

It was only after a few moments that Abuk realized that she didn't want to travel or try anymore. In fact, she felt just like going to sleep and not worrying about things again.

She knew Aben would worry about her, but at the same time she understood that Aben was struggling just to keep herself alive. To care for Abuk meant that there would be less food and water for the older woman. *She will be better off without me to take care of,* Abuk thought to herself.

Ever so slowly, she began losing touch with the things around her. She no longer noticed the heat and the branches above her failed to hold her interest.

It was in that moment that she thought of what Aben had told her about God. "We trust God to provide for us and he will always stay true to his promises."

Well, it now seemed like Aben had been wrong. For months they had struggled just to live. Where was God during those terrible moments of thirst, hunger and loneliness?

Abuk quietly closed her eyes and decided that everything would stop right here, under this large tree. Life had become too hard, with endless struggles and little hope. More than anything else she was tired, exhausted beyond the point of even caring anymore.

Though she wouldn't admit it to herself, Abuk prepared herself for dying. In many ways it was a remarkable thing for a young girl her age to even consider. But given all she had endured in the past and what appeared to be the hopelessness of her future, it was difficult to think of going on. She would just sleep and let things naturally take care of themselves. With little to keep her going, Abuk drifted off into a weary slumber.

Two hours later the sun was spending its last few moments covering the land with a golden hue before it descended beyond the horizon. No one noticed the little girl curled up under the tree with the long branches. For a short time, Abuk no longer felt the pain of hunger or thirst. She slept deeply and yet her energies were nearing their end. With virtually nothing in her stomach for days, life was slowly seeping out of her. Before she even went to sleep, Abuk had known this and accepted her fate.

It was just as the sun shone its last few rays that Abuk, even while fully asleep, had the strangest sensation she was being watched, observed by someone in whose presence she felt warmed.

Suddenly she felt her hand being taken by another person. Her palm was being gently stroked and she felt herself let out a contented sigh.

"Abuk, what are you doing here?" a voiced asked and the words reached far into Abuk's mind. Slowly she started to awaken, even though she felt a strong desire to fall back asleep in the care of this other person.

"Have you given up?" the voice asked and in an instant the little girl recognized the familiar tones.

She slowly opened her eyes and looked on a face she thought she would never see again.

"Mana," she uttered, tears beginning to fill her eyes. And then she asked the next thing that came into her head: "Have I died?"

The face of Abuk's mother broke into a knowing smile. With a slow movement she reached out her hand and gently stroked the dark little face.

"No, my dear, you are still here. But if you don't get up and go back to the village you will not be alive much longer."

Abuk considered this. She curled herself up in her mother's grasp and for a moment the troubles that had haunted her over the last two years faded away. *Why should I go on?* she asked herself. *I have my mother here; this is all I need.*

It was only then that her mind started becoming clearer and she realized that this just couldn't be. Her mother had been killed two years ago by the landmine. If she was dead and Abuk was alive, how could the two of them possibly be in the same place at the same time?

She was about to ask her mother how this could be when the older woman said: "Come, little one, we have much walking to do and there is much for us to speak about."

Abuk picked her body up from the ground but before she could take another step she felt her mother grip her hand firmly.

"What?" the daughter asked.

"O, how I have missed you," her mother responded. "We should start back soon, but let me hold you for a few more minutes."

"O, Mana," Abuk groaned and in an instant fell into her mother's embrace. And in that moment there wasn't enough room in the world to contain all the love expressed between their two hearts and minds.

I Was Always Here

Abuk felt her hand firmly held in her mother's as they journeyed back to the village. They had only been walking for fifteen minutes when Abuk suddenly felt dizzy and sat down on the hard ground. They had been in the middle of talking about what had happened in the last two years when the child felt too weak to continue.

No sooner had she collapsed on the dirt than her mother, who, like Aben, had always been a physically strong woman, seemed to pick her up effortlessly and lay her down in some shade.

Abuk was about to tell her mother of her terrible hunger when she looked up in disbelief as the older woman gave her a plate with hot fish, goat meat and rice. But best of all was the large container of water that her mother pressed to her lips.

The girl drank until she ran out of breath, then she drank more. It was as if she couldn't stop—her body wouldn't let her. She had craved water for days, even weeks, and her hands firmly gripped the container as if by letting it go she wouldn't get water again.

"Oh, Mana, this is so good!" she exclaimed.

Her mother let out a weary sigh before saying, "No child in this difficult world should have to face what you have been through, Abuk."

Abuk laid back and placed her head on the ground as she thought about what her mother had just said.

"But, Mana, there are so many children facing the same thing I am ... I can't even count them all."

The proud face of the older woman gazed at the horizon. "It is this awful war. It has affected everyone and everything in this difficult land of ours. No one escapes it and many don't survive it."

"Will the war ever end?" Abuk asked sadly.

"Yes, dear, and it will end sooner than you think."

Something in the way her mother spoke the words caused the daughter to turn her head and face her directly. Her mother seemed so sure. But how could she know? How could anyone know the future?

It was then that the questions she had asked herself earlier came back into her mind. Abuk had touched her mother's dead body on the ground two years ago; how could she be alive? How did she know where to find her daughter? Where did she get all that delicious food and the abundant supply of water?

"You're not real, are you?" the little girl said at last. "I'm just dreaming this ... I must be."

"Don't be so sure, Abuk," her mother answered quietly. She turned to face her daughter directly and added, "Do you remember all the talks we used to have, just before I put you to bed each night?"

"You mean when you helped me say my prayers?"

"That's right," the older woman smiled. "You used to say that we might be trapped in slavery forever and you wondered why you should have to pray when God didn't seem to care anyway."

Abuk thought about that for a few moments. Those were terrible times, moments when she had waited in vain for God to assist them.

"I still think that way," she responded finally.

Her mother took her hand. "I know you do ... and who can

blame you? But perhaps you have overlooked something very important."

Abuk gave her mother a questioning look.

"You used to pray that God would deliver us from our difficult master and free us from slavery. Abuk, that is exactly what happened—life has been hard for you, but you are free."

"Free!" Abuk blurted. "Mana, I have never been free from hunger or thirst. And do you know what the worst has been? I have never been free of the loneliness I felt after you were gone. How can that be free?"

The tears in the mother's eyes now matched those of her daughter's. Abuk's despair was almost too powerful for the older woman to bear. What could she say to help her daughter to understand? She gripped the girl even tighter as she thought of what to say next.

"Abuk, there are many bondages in life—lack of food and water, poor health, even a lack of love—but the worst kind of all is not being able to choose anything for yourself. That is what we faced in the north and every day I lived in that shame."

Silently, Abuk knew she was right. Her memory flooded with thoughts of the cries of her mother during those nights when the master visited and the anger she felt that nothing could be done about it. Thinking about it now, she realized she had been only considering her own troubles and not those of all those yet trapped in slavery.

"I'm sorry, Mana," she said sadly as she reached up to wipe away her mother's tears. "It has just been so hard. I haven't known what to do about it or who to turn to. Aben has been wonderful to me but even she wonders where our next meal will come from. She talks like you, saying that our God stays faithful to his people, but it doesn't work for her either."

"Are you so sure?" her mother asked.

"I ... I think so."

The woman placed her hand under her daughter's chin and lifted it to face her directly. "How do you think she survived this long, Abuk? God doesn't just supply us with food and drink. Along the way we need those things that are even more essential to the life of our spirits—courage, love, our national pride and, above all, hope. Aben has a deep supply of all of these things and she is rich in those things that truly matter. They are the things that more than anything else God has given to all of us in Sudan—in both the north and the south."

"The north!" exclaimed Abuk. "How can you possibly say that?"

"I know, I know," her mother responded with a smile. I felt much like you, but I have been shown many things since we have been apart. I have learned that the Arab mothers of the north weep for the children they have lost to this awful war. I learned that the Arabs we learned to distrust over all these years have spoken against the slavery practiced by their own government and some have been tortured and jailed as a result. And above all I have learned about the unforgiving spirit that lived in my heart, especially in those years you and I spent in the north."

The mother stopped, struggling to find her next words. When they came, they did so with deep emotion.

"In spite of all the years of war, Abuk, God has kept the true spirit of peace alive in both northerners and southerners. There is much all of us have to overcome and there is much work to do, but the spirit for peace has not died and soon it will bear fruit."

It was all too much for Abuk's young mind to grasp. Instead, she felt overwhelmed by the realities of war that had so desperately shaped her young life.

"You seem ... different, Mana. You never spoke like this before. You always spoke of being free but all this about northerners wanting peace doesn't sound like you. And how can you be so sure that peace is coming soon?"

The mother smiled. "We have much to discuss. I have been in a place where all things are taught well and lessons are learned. And I have understood that the hope residing in the human spirit is stronger than anything hatred can try to undo. It is that hope you must now embrace again, Abuk, because it is God that gives the strength to go on."

Abuk thought about this—it seemed so strange and mysterious. "Mana, where were you? It has been two years and yet you never visited me."

"I have always been here. It is true that I died on that day when we were separated, but God took me to his heart and showed me many things. And he knew you were losing hope and so he sent me back to guide you."

"You are an angel then?" Abuk asked in confusion.

"O, no, little one," the older woman replied. "I am still your mother and I always will be. I cannot be with you like I was, and my time with you might well be brief, but in the time we have I will love you as always. For now, however, I have much to show you."

"You are … dead, but you are here. I can't understand Mana."

"I think you will," her mother responded kindly.

"I know you have much to show me, Mana, but for right now can you just hold me. The sadness in my heart is as great as ever, in spite of all you have said."

In a deep embrace, the two of them hummed together the songs they had learned years ago.

Back to the Village

Aben kept herself busy looking for any spare bits of firewood she could find but she was worried. Abuk had left hours earlier and hadn't returned. Things were becoming desperate and the older woman knew that the little girl was nearing the end of her endurance. She looked up repeatedly in the direction Abuk had wandered, shading her eyes from the setting sun.

And then suddenly she was there, just a small figure in the distance. Aben felt the relief flood through her body and she told herself not to reveal to the girl her sense of worry.

Abuk and her mother spotted Aben at the same moment she saw them. In that moment her mother stopped, touched her shoulder and faced her directly.

"Abuk, it's important not to tell Aben about our last few hours together. I am here to assist you for what will come next. This is something between the two of us. Can we just keep it that way for now? Aben will find out what is happening soon enough."

The girl nodded in agreement yet appeared confused. "What is it?" her mother inquired quietly.

"You said something about helping me 'for what will come next.' What does that mean?"

At this her mother placed her hand on Abuk's cheek. "All in due time, Abuk," she replied. "You have already had so much that is new presented to you today that we should just take things slowly. Do you think you can do that?"

Her daughter thought about this for a moment, then, silently, she took her mother's hand and walked towards the village.

"I see you made your way back all right." In spite of her attempts at busyness, the little girl could sense the emotion in Aben's voice. She felt her heart go out to the older woman when she saw her turn away and wipe her eyes.

"I found something you might like," said Abuk quietly.

Aben took the parcel from Abuk and gently removed the cloth covering. To her shock she saw pieces of fish, goat and a generous helping of rice that the girl had saved from the earlier dinner provided by her mother.

"How? Where did you ever find this?"

Somewhere along the way Abuk had sensed that her mother's physical presence had departed, yet she somehow felt she was still nearby. "It was a present from someone who took pity on us both," was all Abuk would say.

The proud Dinka woman looked questioningly at Abuk, sensing that not all was being explained. Thinking better of asking more, she proceeded to separate the meal into two portions.

"Take it all, Aben. I have already had my fill." Abuk said this with such authority that the older woman silently obeyed, consuming the meal hungrily and realizing that something had happened to the girl since she said goodbye to her in the morning.

After she had eaten the meal but before she could question Abuk further, Aben noticed that she had disappeared inside the tukul, presumably to rest. What she couldn't know was that the girl was feeling deeply saddened.

Her mother had challenged her to be brave and to not lose hope, but at this particular moment she felt herself overcome with a deep sense of loneliness. For so long she had been without her mother, surviving in a world that seemed to become more unbearable with each passing day. And then suddenly she was there, just as Abuk had remembered her, only this time she had seemed even more wise and knowing.

Then just as suddenly her mother had faded from view, leaving the child alone again. The thought of it was almost too much.

She heard Aben rustling outside but chose to stay alone in her thoughts. "Oh, Mana," she pleaded in a whispering voice, "where are you now?"

"I am here, little one, just as I said I would be."

The girl sat up straight, fully surprised to see her mother's figure seated next to her. In a split second she was in her mother's embrace once more and suddenly her loneliness was gone.

In that moment there was nothing to say—only feelings of contentment to be enjoyed. If it is true what they say, that a mother's embrace of her child is perhaps the world's most powerful emotion, then what was being shared in the tukul at that moment was love as it had rarely been felt.

Abuk heard her mother quietly humming, almost as if she was attempting to fly her daughter's spirit away to someplace fully peaceful.

The moment was not to last. A series of explosions could be heard in the distance. These weren't new to Abuk; she had heard them over the years far more frequently than she would have liked. Yet, unlike those other times, she refused to move. Her mother's embrace was strangely comforting.

She heard numerous voices coming from not far away and the more people spoke the more excited their voices became. Eventually they came closer to the tukul and she could hear Aben joining in the conversation.

Then the voices started moving away. She could hear Aben's footsteps approach the tukul and just as quickly as her mother had appeared, she was gone again.

The girl had little time to feel the desperation of loneliness at that moment, for Aben burst in and quickly gathered up the belongings that were in the mud hut.

"Again?" This was the only word that came from Abuk's mouth, but it was immediately understood.

Aben gave out a sigh and paused briefly, looking at Abuk in a forlorn fashion.

"Government forces have broken through our defences and are making their way straight down the railroad tracks towards the village. If our soldiers can't stop them, they should be here within half a day. It's time, Abuk, We must move again."

Her mother, disappeared; Aben in an agitated rush, and moving again, just as she had so many times before—it all left the little girl too weary for effort.

All was quiet for a moment. Then, as explosions came from the distance once more, Aben assisted the girl in standing up, placed a pack on her shoulder, and the two of them headed off in the direction of the village centre.

Once there, they gathered along with everyone else around the Chief of the village. "We must move on to Yargot as soon as we can," he shouted to those assembled. "Our local commander is trying to move our troops into the area as quickly as he can, but they have some distance to come and it is best that we seek safety somewhere else."

Quietly, sadly, everyone followed the Chief as he made his way out of the village and farther to the southeast. This was the story of the Dinka existence—war, famine, constant moving. It had been repeated for over 20 years now and it always brought with it a terrible sense of loss and sadness.

Regardless of where they fled, no place seemed secure. When they tried to get to the larger village of Yargot, their path was always cut off by enemy soldiers who seemed to come out of nowhere.

The Dinka people of south Sudan had become remarkably strong and smart over the many years of conflict. For two decades now they had learned to live with little or no food, under frequent attack from enemy soldiers, and gaining understanding of how to live off the land because nowhere was safe in such a terrible conflict.

One of the things such experiences provided them was an uncanny instinct of knowing how to avoid enemy soldiers. Now that their defenders had portable radios, it became easier for the Dinka to know where enemy troops were placed. Also, many people fleeing from areas where there were attacks would report the locations that were dangerous.

And so, from sunrise to sunset, Abuk and Aben spent their days hiding in riverbeds, swamps or in a growth of trees. When they moved they did so quickly. But instead of being able to journey straight to Yargot, they zigzagged across the country.

Though they occasionally heard the gunfire from enemy soldiers, the hardest part of all for Abuk was the constant sound of enemy helicopters moving across the land. The *whump, whump, whump* of their engines always reminded her of those final moments before her mother stepped on the landmine and her terrible state of loneliness began.

Once in a while they heard of people who had been killed as a result of the fighting. Aben was saddened to learn that an old friend had been killed in a village only a few kilometres distant. Upon discovering that she would see her friend no more, Aben sat under a tree and wondered aloud how much of this war they could all endure. Abuk placed her head on the woman's knee and kept it there in an effort to console her.

Because their own Dinka soldiers were protecting the group of them, there had been enough food to keep everyone alive and travelling. But once those same soldiers moved off, things became desperate again.

To Aben's shock, Abuk began to get very sick. Numerous bite marks from various kinds of bugs convinced her that the girl was suffering from parasites. But when Abuk began to lose weight quickly, it became obvious that something more serious was happening.

Aben had a lengthy discussion with one of the elders and then went to the Chief to determine what to do. "She will not live if we don't get her some medicine," he said sadly. "It would be a shame to see her come through so much just to lose her at a time like now."

Everyone held the same sentiment for, to all of them Abuk had become something of a symbol of the resilience of her own people. They could have left her to die but, instead, they shared their own resources with her, protected her, and ultimately provided Aben to look out for her. The seriousness of the girl's sickness was creating a heavy spirit in the entire group.

"Take her south quickly," the Chief continued. "I have no one to send with you, but there is a clinic near Gordhim. If you can get there, they can assist her."

Aben considered what this would mean. She would be leaving the safety of the group as well as the resources of food and water they all shared sparingly. And if anything should happen, she and Abuk would be defenceless. Yet there was no alternative—Abuk's life mattered more than anything else, including Aben's own safety.

As she prepared Abuk for the difficult journey ahead, Aben was gratified to see the Chief approach her with a number of women. "Take these with you," he said, offering her some extra provisions which had been raised from the others. "We will head to Yargot in the morning. Meet us there when you can."

Abuk's condition was such that Aben decided not to wait until morning. At great risk to both of them, she headed out into the night, holding Abuk's hand and moving instinctively to where she knew the medical clinic would be situated. Fortunately, as with many Sudanese nights, the moon shone brightly, and though she stayed close to the trees along the way, she encountered no enemy soldiers that night.

By morning they were both tired. As they stopped to rest briefly, Abuk slumped into a kind of trance. Her temperature was high and she was obviously having strange dreams. "Mana, Mana, come to me," the child called out repeatedly. "Where are you, Mana?"

Hearing this, Aben thought Abuk must be close to death. Her faith, learned from the elders, had taught her that those about to die return to their ancestors and, together, they join in the presence of God. She had no way of knowing that the child was calling out to a mother she had seen just the day before.

Abuk's body felt very hot and heavy, but her mind felt to her as light as a feather. She kept having different thoughts that at times seemed connected and other times not. Within a brief period of time she would think of her captivity in the north, Aben's kindness, her mother's sudden appearance and the ever-present hunger in her stomach. Though she was suffering thoughts of delirium, her thoughts consistently moved towards her mother.

And then she felt the familiar arms around her. She cuddled into her mother's arms and sought consolation. Abuk never saw her mother's tears but she did feel her love and for the moment that was enough.

"Little one, can you hear me?" When no answer came she tried again. "Abuk, can you hear my voice?"

Quickly the weak voice responded, "Yes, Mana, I can hear you. Why did you take so long to come to me?"

"Aben has been taking good care of you, Abuk. She will get you the help you need," replied her mother.

And then her daughter asked the question that she dreaded to hear: "Mana, am I dying? I feel so ... strange."

"No ... Abuk, don't speak in such a way. You must go on. Listen to Aben. Just a few more hours of walking and there will be people who can help you."

She stroked her daughter's forehead. "Can you do that, Abuk? Will you do as your mother asks?"

Something came across the little girl at that moment. Her mother—the mother she thought she had lost forever—had asked her to be brave and to endure. And for her mother she must do so. With a huge effort she brought herself into a sitting position and tried to think of walking again.

Aben watched in fascination. She neither saw Abuk's mother nor heard her speak, but the child's words were mesmerizing. From somewhere deep within her, Abuk was calling upon her own spirit. If it helped the child to believe she was talking to her mother, then so be it, as long as it helped her to move on a few kilometres more. Once again, Aben had no idea that there were three people seated under the tree in that moment, not two.

In a way that filled Aben with admiration, Abuk summoned up the strength to keep walking, though she occasionally complained of how hot she was.

Towards mid-morning they finally arrived at Gordhim and the medical clinic by the edge of the village. They waited in a long line of people all requiring assistance, but the moment a nurse saw Abuk she brought her inside the cement building to see the doctor.

After a full fifteen minute examination, the doctor turned to Aben, handing her two bottles of pills in the process. "This bottle will help with the parasites," he said, pointing to the smaller of the two vials. "She is also very malnourished; take these pills in the other bottle and they should help."

He then stood to face the woman. "I have no doubt she is suffering from some tuberculosis, but there is nothing I can give you for that—nothing in this clinic anyway. Her real problem is pneumonia; she has it in both lungs and they are full of fluid. That is what is causing her temperature. I am going to give you this third bottle of penicillin, but it is all I have. You must make it last as long as you can. What she requires more than anything else is rest and God only knows how she can get that in this country right now."

Aben was stunned. For some reason the thought of pneumonia had never occurred to her. She herself had experienced it years earlier but had recovered.

As she assisted Abuk in standing, she stood tall, looked down at the doctor, and said in a strong voice: "She will find rest; I will make sure of it."

The doctor and nurse wondered how she could be so sure but they both respected her courage and conviction to do the best for the child.

Fortunately, Aben found an old friend who permitted them to stay in her tukul for the night. After receiving the pills, Abuk slept soundly for the first time in many nights.

Two women watched over Abuk that night—Aben, who determined within herself to get the child to Yargot and to some peace and security, and her mother, who struggled within herself to find a way to prepare her daughter for the days of transition that were about to come.

A Special Journey

Regardless of where they fled, no place seemed secure. When they tried to get to the larger village of Yargot, their path was always cut off by enemy soldiers who seemed to come out of nowhere.

The Dinka people of south Sudan had become remarkably strong and smart over the many years of conflict. For two decades they had learned to live with little or no food, under frequent attack from enemy soldiers and learning to live off the land because nowhere was safe in such a terrible conflict.

One of the things such experiences provided them was an uncanny instinct of knowing how to avoid enemy soldiers. Now that their defenders had portable radios, it became easier for the Dinka to know where enemy troops were placed. Also, many people fleeing from areas where there were attacks would report the locations that were dangerous.

And so, from sunrise to sunset, Abuk and Aben spent their days hiding in riverbeds, swamps or in a growth of trees. When they moved they did so quickly. But instead of being able to journey straight to Yargot, they zigzagged across the country.

Though they occasionally heard the gunfire from enemy soldiers, the hardest part of all for Abuk was the constant sound of enemy helicopters moving across the land. The *whump, whump* of their engines always reminded her of those final moments before her mother stepped on the landmine and her terrible state of loneliness began.

Once in a while they heard of people who had been killed as a result of the fighting. Aben was saddened to learn that an old friend had been killed in a village only a few kilometres distant. Upon discovering that she would see her friend no more, Aben sat under a tree and wondered aloud how much of this war they could all endure. Abuk placed her head on the woman's knee and kept it there in an effort to console her.

Because their own Dinka soldiers were protecting the group of them, there had been enough food to keep everyone alive and traveling. But once those same soldiers moved off, things became desperate again.

To Aben's shock, Abuk began to get very sick. Numerous bite marks from various kinds of bugs convinced her that the girl was suffering from parasites. But when Abuk began to lose weight quickly, it became obvious that something more serious was happening.

Aben had a lengthy discussion with one of the elders and then went to the Chief to determine what to do. "She will not live if we don't get her some medicine," he said sadly. "It would be a shame to see her come through so much just to lose her at a time like now."

Everyone held the same sentiment for, to all of them, Abuk had become something of a symbol of the resilience of her own people. They could have left her to die but, instead, they shared their own resources with her, protected her, and ultimately provided Aben to look out for her. The seriousness of the girl's sickness was creating a heavy spirit in the entire group.

"Take her south quickly," the Chief continued. "I have no one to send with you, but there is a clinic near Gordhim. If you can get there, they can assist her."

Aben considered what this would mean. She would be leaving the safety of the group as well as the resources of food and water they all shared sparingly. And if anything should happen, she and Abuk would be defenceless. Yet there was no alternative—Abuk's life mattered more than anything else, including Aben's own safety.

As she prepared Abuk for the difficult journey ahead, Aben was gratified to see the Chief approach her with a number of women. "Take these with you," he said, offering her some extra provisions which had been raised from the others. "We will head to Yargot in the morning. Meet us there when you can."

Abuk's condition was such that Aben decided not to wait until morning. At great risk to both of them, she headed out into the night, holding Abuk's hand and moving instinctively to where she knew the medical clinic would be situated. Fortunately, as with many Sudanese nights, the moon shone brightly, and though she stayed close to the trees along the way, she encountered no enemy soldiers that night.

By morning they were both tired. As they stopped to rest briefly, Abuk slumped into a kind of trance. Her temperature was high and she was obviously having strange dreams. "Mana, Mana, come to me," the child called out repeatedly. "Where are you, Mana?"

Hearing this, Aben thought Abuk must be close to death. Her faith, learned from the elders, had taught her that those about to die return to their ancestors and, together, they join in the presence of God. She had no way of knowing that the child was calling out to a mother she had seen just the day before.

Abuk's body felt very hot and heavy, but her mind felt to her as light as a feather. She kept having different thoughts that at times seemed connected and, other times, not. Within a brief period of time she would think of her captivity in the north, Aben's kindness, her mother's sudden appearance and the ever-present hunger in her stomach. Though she was suffering thoughts of delirium, those thoughts consistently moved towards her mother.

then she felt the familiar arms around her. She cuddled into her mother's arms and sought consolation. Abuk never saw her mother's tears but she did feel her love and for the moment that was enough.

"Little one, can you hear me?" When no answer came she tried again. "Abuk, can you hear my voice?"

Quickly the weak voice responded, "Yes, Mana, I can hear you. Why did you take so long to come to me?"

"Aben has been taking good care of you, Abuk. She will get you the help you need," replied her mother.

And then her daughter asked the question that she dreaded to hear: "Mana, am I dying? I feel so … strange."

"No … Abuk, don't speak in such a way. You must go on. Listen to Aben. Just a few more hours of walking and there will be people who can help you."

She stroked her daughter's forehead. "Can you do that, Abuk? Will you do as your mother asks?"

Something came across the little girl at that moment. Her mother—the mother she thought she had lost forever—had asked her to be brave and to endure. And for her mother she must do so. With a huge effort she brought herself into a sitting position and tried to think of walking again.

Aben watched in fascination. She neither saw Abuk's mother nor heard her speak, but the child's words were mesmerizing. From somewhere deep within her, Abuk was calling upon her own spirit. If it helped the child to believe she was talking to her mother, then so be it, as long as it helped her to move on a few kilometres more. Once again, Aben had no idea that there were three people seated under the tree in that moment, not two.

In a way that filled Aben with admiration, Abuk summoned up the strength to keep walking, though she occasionally complained of how hot she was.

Towards mid-morning they finally arrived at Gordhim and the medical clinic by the edge of the village. They waited in a long line of people all requiring assistance, but the moment a nurse saw Abuk she brought her inside the cement building to see the doctor.

After a full fifteen minute examination, the doctor turned to Aben, handing her two bottles of pills in the process. "This bottle will help with the parasites," he said, pointing to the smaller of the two vials. "She is also very malnourished; take these pills in the other bottle and they should help."

He then stood to face the woman. "I have no doubt she is suffering from some tuberculosis, but there is nothing I can give you for that—nothing in this clinic anyway. Her real problem is pneumonia; she has it in both lungs and they are full of fluid. That is what is causing her temperature. I am going to give you this third bottle of penicillin, but it is all I have. You must make it last as long as you can. What she requires more than anything else is rest and God only knows how she can get that in this country right now."

Aben was stunned. For some reason the thought of pneumonia had never occurred to her. She herself had experienced it years earlier but had recovered.

As she assisted Abuk in standing, she stood tall, looked down at the doctor, and said in a strong voice: "She will find rest; I will make sure of it."

The doctor and nurse wondered how she could be so sure but they both respected her courage and conviction to do the best for the child.

Fortunately, Aben found an old friend who permitted them to stay in her tukul for the night. After receiving the pills, Abuk slept soundly for the first time in many nights.

Two women watched over Abuk that night—Aben, who determined within herself to get the child to Yargot and to some peace and security, and her mother, who struggled within herself to find a way to prepare her daughter for the days of transition that were about to come.

The Package

Aben was fully determined to do whatever it took to get the young girl to Yargot. Though Abuk appeared better the next day, she knew it would only be short-lived, unless she was able to find her some peace and quiet. Who knew where the enemy soldiers might be on the way? What if Yargot was unapproachable?

A strong woman whose spiritual faith matched her physical strength, she used every resource she had to get the child to safety.

It turned out she needn't have worried. As she neared Yargot, she noticed many others travelling in the same direction. "Our troops beat back the invaders," one woman told her. "They are now far away."

Sure enough, Aben sensed the relief the moment she came near the village. Speaking with others near a well, she discovered that the enemy forces had indeed killed a number of people and taken away cattle, goats or anything else they could get their hands on. But as the conflict wore on, more fighters from other villages arrived to drive back the enemy soldiers. Though the struggle had taken two entire days, the region was now at peace—at least until the next attack.

Aben also discovered some other information that made her curious. The commissioner for the entire area had arrived at Yargot and was on his way to Aben's tukul. She had no way of knowing what someone that important would want with her.

"Did he say what he wanted?" she asked.

"No," a young boy replied. "All he said was that he had something special for you and the child with you."

"The child!" Aben said forcefully. "What would he possibly have to say to Abuk?" The thought continued to occupy her mind as she made her way back to Abuk.

She had left the little girl in the care of a friend while she went to search for water, but now as she returned she could see that Abuk didn't seem to be responding well to the medication.

"She continues to talk to her mother," the friend said. "It's almost like she is dreaming that her mother is here in the tukul."

This wasn't new to Aben, as she had repeatedly heard the girl speaking to "Mana" the last day or so. Even now, as she bent down to feel the girl's forehead she had the distinct impression that Abuk looked like she was curled up in someone's lap.

"Abuk. Abuk. It's time for more of your medication. Come on, sit up."

The little girl opened her weary eyes and attempted to do what Aben asked, but she was so weak she required assistance.

"Here, I have ground this pill up for you—take it with this water. It will help your lungs to feel better."

Suffering a high temperature, Abuk looked for her mother and was saddened to see she was gone. "Mana," she cried quietly, causing Aben to become even more concerned.

Shortly after taking the pill, Abuk fell asleep once more. As Aben and her friend stood outside the tukul, the friend said: "It is almost like her time with us is brief, Aben. She is calling to her mother because she is dying."

Aben looked up fiercely but in the end looked away because her friend had only spoken the truth. Try as she might, she couldn't help

Abuk to get stronger. The community had placed the child in her care and she had not been able to keep the terrible effects of war and disease from hurting the girl.

Leaving her friend to be alone for a while, she uttered, "Surely her mother would have done a better job than I. I have failed her, my village and Abuk."

The sudden realization completely devastated her as she knelt by a tree and wept. For someone as strong and spirited as this woman, such moments were rare. Aben had lost many loved ones to the war, so she was not a stranger to death. But somehow Abuk had been different. She was like a gift from God—a gift that had filled her own life with meaning and hope. Now that the little girl was weakening she felt her own hope fading in the process.

She had only been crying a few minutes when she felt a hand on her shoulder. She looked up, startled to see the compassionate face of a woman roughly the same age who had obviously seen her own share of pain and suffering.

"Here, drink this water; it will help," the woman said.

Aben obediently did as she was told.

"I overheard you say that you had failed and I just wondered if that was really true?"

How did she hear that? Aben asked herself before replying, "It has just been too much. Abuk was my special charge, my responsibility, but I could not compete against this war. It has finally beaten me."

The words were so heart-felt that the woman held Aben in a compassionate embrace. "You have kept her alive. You got her to a clinic and then here to Yargot. That took much strength and determination."

"And I prayed," Aben sobbed, responding to the woman's kind words. "I prayed that God would give me the resources needed to keep her alive and I failed."

"Do you have water?" asked the woman.

"Yes," Aben replied.

"Food?"

"Some, but not much."

"And you have medicine and a tukul to keep Abuk sheltered in?"

Aben only nodded this time as she waited for what the woman would say next.

"Then what resources did you fail to acquire?" she asked finally.

In an instant Aben realized the woman was right. They were safe, sheltered and fed. More importantly, there was at least some medicine for the next couple of days.

Wiping away her tears, Aben lifted herself up as she brushed the dust from her clothes. She turned to thank the kind woman only to discover that she had quietly left. Aben looked in the direction of the village but couldn't spot the woman anywhere.

But something had changed inside her as a result of the conversation. As of yet Abuk was still alive—Aben had done at least that much. And somewhere deep within her came the sense that she must continue one day at a time to preserve the little life. With a new sense of determination she began to prepare herself for what she had to do next.

"Almost there," Aben said with a sense of enthusiasm in her voice.

"Where?" Abuk asked weakly.

"Home."

Sure enough, as Abuk lifted her gaze, she saw the familiar cornfield that now stood between them and the tukul that had served as their home for the last number of years.

Somehow, in her little heart, she had yearned for this place over the last few days. The closer she got to the tukul the more she felt calmed and content.

When Aben opened the flap to the tukul they were both completely unprepared for what they saw. On a makeshift shelf along the one wall were a number of cans of Cerelac, along with some other food items. They were both overwhelmed by what was before them.

"Aben, who? How?" Abuk asked. The older woman had no answer but she wasn't about to waste the moment.

"Here, lie down for a minute while I prepare some of this for you," she said to Abuk.

"You, too," the girl pleaded. "Make some for yourself."

The truth was that Aben was far too excited to eat. In the tukul was enough food to assist Abuk for some time—a huge burden had suddenly lifted from her shoulders. With an old knife she opened the can of meal and began to mix it with the water.

"Hello, are you there Aben?"

She knew immediately it was the voice of the village Chief. "Come in … enter," she said to the voice outside.

But instead of just one person, the Chief entered with two other people from the village, their arms full of clothing.

"The commissioner was by this morning, looking for you and the little one. He brought a large package full of this food in front of you … and these."

He motioned for the other two to dump the clothing on the wooden table. Aben discovered different kinds of clothing, from shorts and tops to a small pair of sandals. Compared to Abuk's rags they were the nicest clothes the woman had ever seen.

"And there is this," the Chief said behind her.

She turned to find him holding up two other items of clothing, only much larger. "These are for you," he said quietly.

"Me? Why?" was all she could think to say.

She took the beige skirt that was knee-length and pleated in the back. And with it came a sleeveless blue polka-dot top, of a pattern she had never seen before. She pulled them to her face and breathed deeply, delighting in the freshness of the scent.

"These came all the way from Canada, from a special woman who wants you to know she is aware of your condition … and Abuk's." His last two words caused her to look at the child on the ground who was gazing at the clothes with fascination. Something in the way he said those words sent a sudden excitement through her spirit.

"We have much to talk about," said the Chief.

The Conversation

It was a few moments before Aben could utter the word which the Chief had just used.

"Adoption?" she finally said.

"It's true," continued the Chief. "Somehow she heard of Abuk's story many months ago and has been trying to locate her ever since."

"Does she live here?"

"No, but she does come here occasionally to assist our people in fleeing slavery. She and her husband are true friends of our people, Aben, and we shouldn't consider the request lightly. However, I would wish to take your own feelings into account."

What could she say? The momentous importance of the request was something none of her people had experienced before. Children lived or often died in this country and no one had ever considered that some outside source could actually assist. Food and clothing had often been flown in to assist the children, but no one ever thought that a child could actually go to another country.

How could she describe her own feelings right now? The story seemed incredible yet obviously the Chief treated it with great seriousness. Like all others in her village she held the Chief in the highest respect. He had successfully distributed what little resources there were equally amongst all the village. His compassionate decision about the community caring for Abuk once her mother had died was probably the one main reason the girl was still alive.

She knew the difficult sensation in her heart right now was nothing other than a kind of jealousy. After all, wasn't it she who had watched over Abuk all these difficult years? Had she not given to the child the food that would normally be for her? Wasn't it Aben who had risked her own life for the sake of the younger child? If Aben really was jealous, didn't she have a right to be?

Full of conflicting emotions she turned to the Chief and spoke firmly: "I need some time to think about this. It is too important to expect me to come to some decision in a few moments."

He looked to the ground, nodding in agreement. "You are right, Aben. You of all of us here have the most at stake over this decision. Spend the night thinking about this situation and I will return with the other village elders in the morning. I am sorry to have laid this burden on you in such a fashion."

The Chief walked away quietly and Aben thought once again of how lucky they all were to have such a humble and generous leader. Nevertheless, he was right. It was her decision and she knew she would have to make it soon.

When she went back inside the tukul she was relieved to see that Abuk was asleep, probably from exhaustion. This provided Aben some much needed time to think about what should be done next.

She went outside and began to boil some water on a small but smokey fire. Each time it threatened to go out she took a hollow reed and continued to blow gently on the coals. Eventually it was able to sustain the flames on its own strength and she prepared some tea for herself.

At that moment a great pang of hunger seized her and she thought of the storehouse of food that sat on the shelves in the tukul, provided by the woman in Canada. In that instant Aben did what she had always done since the first hour she was placed in charge of

Abuk—she decided to leave the food where it was so that it would last Abuk longer. It was for this kind of generosity and sacrifice that the village has instinctively known that Aben would be the best person to watch over the child.

Moments later, as she sipped her hot tea, she thought again of how much she had sacrificed for the child and thought it only fair that she remain in charge of Abuk. But the more she thought of Canada the more her heart pulled her in another direction.

In truth, Aben knew hardly anything about that faraway land. She had heard somewhere that it was like America and that it was a place of great wealth and prosperity.

And there was one more thing that she knew about it. Day after day it had partly been the food supplied by the Government of Canada that had been dropped from the large planes in the sky that kept the southern Sudanese people alive.

For these reasons Aben could only think of Canada as someplace wonderful, wealthy and compassionate. Would Abuk ever suffer there? Could she not get a full education and make enough money to keep herself?

But then she thought once again of how she would miss this child she had taken into her own heart. Clearly, Aben's feelings were torn and the more she thought about it the more desolate she became.

It was then that she saw the form of a woman making her way past the tukul. Somehow Aben knew that it was the woman she had spoken to earlier who had shown such kindness. As the woman walked past Aben called out quietly, "Would you like some tea?"

A smile crossed the woman's lips, almost as if she had known Aben would ask. "Please, thank you," she responded.

As the woman sat next to her, Aben felt herself strangely drawn to her. They sipped their tea in silence before the stranger spoke.

"You seem to be troubled," she observed.

Aben only nodded in agreement, unsure as to what to say next.

"It seems as though troubled thoughts and difficult decisions always plague our people," the woman said. "Hardship becomes such a way of life that we want to steal whatever joy we can from this world before it all gets snatched away again. This is how we think as a people."

The woman was right, Aben knew. Aben and Abuk had known nothing but destitution since they had been together and she understood that such was the life of all in south Sudan. This woman knew that.

"Decisions in such a world are always the most difficult," the woman added.

Aben had the odd feeling this stranger understood all that had passed in the last hour. But how could she know that Aben faced one of the crucial decisions of her life?

"At times … at times one wants to take what one can when the opportunity is there," Aben said to her.

"And so we should. There are so few opportunities for us women to find joy." Aben suddenly felt a sense of relief, feeling that Abuk could continue to be that joy for her.

"Except …"

"Except what?" Aben asked, prodding her to continue.

"Except when it comes to life itself. It is a gift of God and even our joy at times must bow before it. We understand this better than most women in this troubled world," observed the woman quietly.

Aben was now fully curious. "What do you mean that life must come before joy?"

"Why do you think it is that Sudanese women never find the

joy they deserve?" the woman asked. Before Aben could reply she continued. "It is because our greatest calling is to sacrifice our own wants to the needs of those most dear to us. They come first—they always come first. We have forever known this in our heart of hearts."

Aben sighed, adding, "It is why we are the most cursed of all women."

To her surprise the stranger raised her voice while she pointed at Aben. "Never say that … never," she said. "It is because of this that we are the most blessed of all women. Our own faith tells of Mary, the mother of Jesus, and how she willingly sacrificed her own peace and comfort to provide her son with the support he needed. Jesus sacrificed himself for all people, choosing to leave his own welfare to God. Even Muhammad, the great prophet of Islam, spoke of sacrificing his peaceful life for the betterment of his people. We don't like to think of our enemies in the north worshipping such a prophet, but they do because it is universally true that the best life to live is the life that empties itself out for others. For this reason we are the most blessed of women in this world. Never deny it."

The strength of the woman's words overwhelmed Aben. And the wisdom of her thoughts made Aben feel somewhat ashamed of how she had considered her own welfare ahead of Abuk's. "I just desired to share my time with someone who has brought me much meaning in my life."

"I know … I know," the woman said as she started to stand. "But the real question we must all ask is what is best for the one we love. It is from how we answer such challenges that the world will know the true dignity of our people. Rest your heart now, for you already know the answer to your question."

She placed her hand in Aben's own briefly and then made her way down the path. She is the spirit of all our people, Aben thought to herself. But who was she and how did she understand what Aben had been struggling with?

It didn't matter, for in that instant Aben knew the woman was right—the answer was now clear to her. With this in mind, she did what Sudanese women always do and, as she carried her sadness into the tukul, she thought about how to assist young Abuk in embracing the opportunity that would be set before her and that would forever alter her future.

Two Futures

So much to eat. Abuk opened her eyes the next morning to see the shelves lined with food items. She turned her head and spotted the small sandals that were meant just for her. Slowly she placed her feet in the straps and did up the buckles.

For the first time in her entire life the young girl had something to cover the soles of her feet. Calloused from years of walking, her soles were cracked and dried and the moment she put the sandals on her feet they felt different but better.

She considered for some time where all these provisions had come from and her young mind concluded that somehow the village, and perhaps the Chief especially, had come upon a large store of supplies from some foreign relief agency. The fact that all these gifts had come from just one person in a faraway land did not occur to her, nor could she even comprehend such a possibility.

She emerged from the tukul's opening and caught Aben eyeing her closely. Abuk stretched her arms out at her sides and motioned for the woman to look down at the ground.

Aben gazed at the sandals covering the feet and gave a quick nod of approval, much to Abuk's delight. But as Aben took a second look she felt some alarm at the sheer thinness of the child's legs—never had she looked so skinny. Nevertheless, this wasn't the moment to reveal such concern. Instead she summoned Abuk into her embrace and said, "They look so beautiful on you."

Abuk beamed in satisfaction. "Can I try on some of the clothes before we do our chores? I promise I'll get them done today."

"Actually, there will be no chores today, Abuk. Lets try on all that is there, then I'll make a big meal. There is something I want to talk to you about and the chores can wait until tomorrow."

Abuk missed the seriousness in Aben's tone, choosing instead to express her delight at having to do no work for the day. In a blur, she burst back inside the tukul and began trying on one outfit after another.

Later, they sat in front of the dying fire eating the last bits of the creamed potatoes and canned beans that had been sitting on the shelf only a few minutes before. Aben couldn't recall the last time she had seen the child look so satisfied, so much like a carefree little girl.

In truth, Abuk was living in something like a dream. The grim realities around her never intruded on this new world she had discovered. Gone was the hunger and the lack of clothing. Suddenly she was in a world of warmth and happiness.

Seeing her smiling face, Aben was hesitant to discuss with Abuk the new realities she would now have to face. But the sheer delight on the child's face caused her to wait a few more minutes before talking to her. Instead, the two of them sang some songs and held hands as they danced one of the favourite dances of the village. Only when Abuk grew weary from effort did the time seem right for Aben.

"The clothes give you a wonderful feeling, don't they?" she asked finally.

"They don't look … real," Abuk said. And indeed they didn't. The pastel colours and light material were nothing like the clothes worn in south Sudan. For that very reason they had made Abuk feel special and different.

"They are real and they are a special gift, just for you."

The child had already sensed this to be true but she didn't know where they had come from. Quietly she asked, "How did they get here, to our tukul?"

Aben sighed before saying, "It is a long story, Abuk, but one you must listen to very carefully."

Abuk pulled her knees up to her chin and sat on the ground gazing openly at the older woman. The very innocence in her eyes almost made Aben weep.

"Why do you think these clothes and all the food came here just for you?"

"And the sandals, don't forget the sandals," Abuk said, lifting one of her legs to show off her foot.

"Yes, and the sandals too," Aben added. "Why are they just for you?"

Abuk had no idea and merely shook her head from side to side.

"You have heard of Canada, right?" asked Aben.

"I know they give our people food when they are starving."

"That's true, but do you know what Canada is?"

"Another country, I think," said Abuk hesitantly.

"It is another place far, far away, Abuk, and it is filled with people of fairer skin and hair. Somehow they have heard of how our people suffer and they are trying to help."

"Why don't they just come here then, instead of sending things in airplanes?"

The question caught Aben off-guard. "The government in the north restricts them from entering our borders. But some do get through. And there is one special person, maybe two, who are trying very hard to come and see us from Canada. One is the woman who sent you all these things."

Try as she might, Abuk couldn't understand what Aben was attempting to say. Why would these people come just for them? "Do you know them?" she asked finally.

"No, but they have heard of you. In fact they heard of you over a year ago and were determined to help you. These new clothes and food spent months getting here—that's how long they have thought of you."

"Me? Why?" asked Abuk as she studied her sandals once more.

Suddenly Aben didn't know quite what to say or how to continue. This was the very moment she dreaded and yet desired at the same time.

"What would you think about going to Canada, Abuk? Wouldn't you like to see a different place, a country that is free and where you can eat all you want?"

"More than anything I'd like to go to school. Do they have those in Canada?"

"They even have big universities where you can go to become a lawyer or a doctor," Aben said.

"I'd like that … very much."

"Abuk, the man and woman from Canada want to take you there with them, to live with them."

At first Aben thought the child didn't hear her, but then Abuk looked at her directly, asking, "But why would I do that, Aben—this is my home?"

"This will always be your birthplace, child, but right now it is no place for a child to grow up. You have seen for yourself what happens in this place to children."

"Like Yar?" Abuk asked quietly, remembering her friend who had died of hunger over a year ago.

"Yes, like Yar. And that could be you, too, little one. What will we do when the food runs out or if you keep getting sicker? There will be no chance for you here."

It was then that Abuk said the words that stunned the older woman. "My mother died here, Aben, and this is where she would want me to stay. I am her daughter, a child of Sudan, and I will die here as she did, however that happens. And I will stay and take care of you."

Aben stared at her in silence, wondering how one so young should seem so wise. "Oh, Abuk, I will be fine. And your mother would want you to go to where you would have the best chance to live in peace."

"Do you really know that, Aben? Really?"

Aben was unprepared to answer because in truth she didn't know. Like any woman in Sudan, Abuk's mother would want the best for her child, yet she couldn't say for certain.

"Abuk, this Canadian couple will care for you and love you as much as ...as-"

"As you?"

How could they? Aben asked herself. But then she recalled just how easy it was to love this special child. The entire village had sensed it and surely the couple from another country would as well—she was sure of it. "I ... I think they would," she said at last.

"I will not go, Aben. This is my home and I want to take care of you as you get older. These people should not want to take me away from those duties. My love for you is more important than my education or my happiness."

How like a Sudanese woman, Aben thought to herself as she watched the child take off the sandals and walk back into the tukul.

Difficult Decisions

Abuk's remarkable ability to survive was partly due to the same sense of decisiveness and determination she had just shown Aben. She knew her own mind and showed a great maturity at following through on her decisions.

And so she had no doubts to trouble her as she proceeded to put away the clothes that had been laid out around the interior of the tukul. She had no idea what the woman in Canada was like, but she did know Aben and she was determined to remain in Sudan with her.

While the child occupied herself inside, Aben stood by the smouldering fire wondering what she should do next. There were times when she and Abuk had strongly disagreed, but never over something as important as this. Part of the difficulty, she understood, was that Abuk had no conception of what Canada was like or the more prosperous life that would await her there. For that matter, neither did Aben. How then could she make it real to her, real enough to make the important decision to leave Sudan?

Unknown to either of them a powerful influence was soon to overpower the child's confidence and solve the disagreement between them.

"The sandals are beautiful on you, Abuk."

The words fully surprised the girl, who quickly turned to see where the voice was coming from. "Mana!" she exclaimed. "I wondered if you would come back."

"I told you I would be with you to help you with what is to come, Abuk, and I will," her mother answered.

Her daughter felt a quiet fear in her heart as she heard the words "what is to come."

"I've missed you," she said finally.

Her mother smiled a beautiful smile before saying, "I saw you not too long ago."

Wondering why her mother was there, Abuk motioned to the food and clothing. "These have come from a woman in Canada."

"I know. A woman and a man who both care about you."

"How do you know that? Were you listening?"

"I knew many months ago, Abuk. It's why I am here."

It was as Abuk had suspected. "You think I should go with them … I knew you would feel that way."

Her mother assisted her in arranging things on a shelf before saying, "If you knew I thought you should go, why are you fighting me then? Do you not want what's best for you?"

The girl stopped and stared at the shelf in front of her. Finally she turned and there was impatience in her eyes. "I know what's best for me," she asserted. "It was you, Mana, who used to tell me to be proud that I would be a woman of Sudan. Aben tells me that too. And I am proud of it. Aben and you—both of you are brave and I want to be just like that."

Her mother sighed before walking over and holding her daughter tenderly from behind. Slowly she started the rocking motion that often helped Abuk to calm down her emotions.

"You are right. I did tell you that, Abuk. But I told you other things too. I told you that a woman must be strong if she wants to help her country. And more than anything, I told you that nothing will come of all our courage if we don't also use our minds. We must educate ourselves if we are to determine the course of our own lives, but often so little is available to us in this place. Even our men are lucky to get schooling."

"I don't need schooling," Abuk shot back. "I learn fast and I'm just as smart as any of the other young people."

Mana slowly turned her daughter around and lifted her chin so that they looked directly at one another. "You are the smartest child I know, Abuk, but perhaps you are not as intelligent as you think."

"What does that mean?"

"How sick do you think you really are, child?" asked her mother quietly.

Abuk wanted to answer immediately but her mother had spoken to something that was in fact troubling the girl. She had known for some time that her body was getting weaker. It wasn't just the tiredness or hunger. Something in her no longer felt right. Her lungs increasingly felt as though they were on fire and even when she did eat well, as in the last couple of days, the vital food didn't seem to make anything better.

In truth, she knew she was dying, had known it for some time, and yet she couldn't bring herself to admit it. She had attempted to put it out of her mind but her mother's searching questions helped her to realize that it couldn't be hidden any more. With a sigh, she felt tears brimming up in her eyes as she looked despairingly at Mana.

"I know I have the kind of sickness I won't recover from," she admitted quietly.

To her shock, Abuk watched her mother turn away, her hands to her face. The sound of weeping was unmistakable.

"Mana … Mana," she cried out, attempting to turn her mother to face her. "I'm sorry, Mana. What have I done?"

With surprising strength her mother grabbed her shoulders. "Do you know how hard it has been for me to watch you slowly wasting away over the past months. I wanted to come to you but I couldn't—not until the time was right."

"Time? What do you mean?"

"Listen to me," Mana said directly. "I struggled long and hard to keep you alive once you were born. I gave you all the food I had and endured much pain to keep you. But, Abuk, more than anything I wanted you to have freedom—the ability to grow and become a strong woman of Sudan."

She was quiet for a moment before continuing. "But even in my own heart I knew it was hopeless. I knew I couldn't save you."

"Mana, what are you saying?" Abuk cried. "You always told me to hope and that God would answer our prayers."

"I know … I know," her mother whispered. "I tried to be strong—for you—but in my heart I despaired. Even when I took our chance for freedom I wondered what I would be bringing you to. Things were more desperate here than in the north."

Mana was outwardly crying now, causing Abuk to grip her as tightly as she could. It seemed like a long time before words were said again.

"Abuk, after the blast that took me away from you years ago, I felt God telling me to have faith and that something wonderful was in store for you. But to hear you speak like this, to deny even your own future, breaks my heart."

And just like that, suddenly it all became clear to Abuk. Her mother had endured much doubt and sadness, fighting for the hope that perhaps her child, this child, might have more fortune than many other children of the south. All that her mother had done was designed to give her daughter a fighting chance at finding her potential.

And what was Abuk doing about it? Fighting it, going against all that Mana had attempted.

Abuk felt ashamed and embarrassed. Though unwilling to admit it yet, she understood that her mother had given up her own life for such a lofty ideal. She now knew what she had to do.

"Mana … Mana," she said softy, causing the older woman to face her. "I understand—I think. I am not afraid to die but I know that if I stay, nothing that Aben or you can do can keep me from it. But I am afraid, Mana. Where will I go? What will it be like? What about Aben … and you? Will I see you both again? Will I have to go to hospital? Will it be painful? What if this couple from Canada doesn't like me? How will I …?"

Quietly, her mother put her finger over the girl's lips. "I don't know all the answers to these questions, little one, but I know that going to Canada will give you a chance for life and learning."

"But I have a mother—you," Abuk blurted. "I don't want another one."

Once again, her mother broke into tears, but this time kept gazing at her child. "We must talk more about this, Abuk. But for now it is enough that you are willing to go to a strange place in order to find your life. I don't know, but I don't think it will be as difficult as you might suppose There is beauty and courage outside of Sudan. Canada has its own share of these values. But you will always be Sudanese, here in your heart."

As she pointed to the young girl's chest, Abuk jumped into her arms. "I know, I know, Mana. But I will always be your daughter."

"Always …. Always," came the teary reply.

The Moment of Truth

Aben remained unaware of what had taken place in the tukul between Abuk and her mother. What she did know was that the girl seemed to be more delusional than earlier. Not knowing of Mana's presence, Aben assumed Abuk had been merely talking to herself, perhaps in something of a feverish state. The more she heard the girl's mumbling inside, the more she became convinced that Abuk's time on the earth was short.

The girl suddenly emerged from the opening appearing sad and quiet. "Something to eat?" Aben asked quietly but only received a shaking of the head in reply.

Abuk seemed troubled, as though she had something to say. Yet she remained quiet, sitting on a piece of wood and staring into the distance.

"I'm sorry about the trouble I gave you earlier."

They were the words Aben had prayed for. In truth, the disagreement between the two of them had been more painful than usual because of Abuk's deteriorating condition. In a moment Abuk had swept the sadness away.

"These are difficult times," Aben said finally. "It takes all of our energy to just find food and water. There is little energy left for anything else."

What Abuk said next stunned the older woman.

"I hear that Canada has lakes bigger than anything we could imagine. They also have stores where you can find food of any kind, even frozen things."

"How … how do you know that?" Aben blurted.

"I just hear things," came the soft reply.

Neither one knew what to say next. Though an uncomfortable moment, there was something about it that seemed to speak of importance.

"Why are you thinking about Canada?" asked Aben.

"The man and woman who sent the food are from Canada, aren't they? Maybe it would be someplace that could help me and give me schooling."

To Aben it was as though the sun had suddenly broken through dark clouds. But how had Abuk made the journey between refusing to even discuss Canada to her willingness to consider going there? Occasionally the girl had the potential to fully surprise Aben and this was one of those times.

Slowly, Aben knelt on the ground close to Abuk and began fanning the flames of a fire. "Do you want to go?" she asked finally.

Abuk looked at her, eyes brimming with tears. "No, not at all. But what will become of me if I can't get a doctor's help? And how can I help our people if I can't even read or write? If Canada is the kind of place you have said, then it can help me get these things."

"That it can," Aben responded happily. "But you will need someone to look after you, to care for you, and to pay for all these things you speak of."

"I know … I know—the Canadian couple," Abuk responded with a sigh.

Something has happened, Aben thought to herself. Clearly something had taken place in the girl's life in the last few hours that had caused her to make an important journey in her mind. And in typical Abuk fashion, the girl, once she had made a decision, was moving ahead with remarkable speed. Yet Aben couldn't help wondering again how Abuk had changed her mind so quickly. Unaware that Mana had been talking with Abuk in the tukul, Aben just assumed that the girl had come to her senses and understood the need to move along with her life. Nevertheless, regardless of how it came about, Aben was now filled with a certain excitement. There was much to do in the next while and it all depended upon a couple from a faraway country whom she had never met before.

"I'm sure they're nice."

Abuk hardly heard Aben's words. Sitting around the fire in the dark, her thoughts turned to how she could possibly say goodbye to a land and a people she had come to treasure. And what would become of Aben? The girl instinctively understood that in many ways the woman's life would suddenly become much easier. Yet they had become inseparable over the last few years. And Sudan could be a terribly lonely place when there was no companionship to help one through the lack of water, security and food.

"They must be compassionate to have tried so hard to locate you," said Aben, interrupting the girl's thoughts again.

"They are definitely determined," Abuk replied, a little too harshly. Immediately she felt ashamed of her tone.

Aben simply placed a hand on her shoulder to signal that she understood the girl's discomfort. It was so much for a young mind to grasp, especially because of her deteriorating physical condition. The girl appeared deathly ill now, in much deeper pain than any time Aben had seen in the past.

"Do you think they'll have a house?" asked Abuk, as a way of making things better.

"From what I've heard, everyone in Canada has a house. They have huge roads that travel over the horizon on which you can drive days and days without ever leaving the country. And, like here, they have huge pieces of land that no one lives on. And then there's all that snow."

For a brief moment the girl permitted herself a smile. "I have heard about snow from one of the teachers at the mission school a few years ago. It is white, cold, and melts in your hands if you try to squeeze it."

They both laughed at the thought of it. "How can something that is solid disappear into nothing?" Aben commented.

"I will find out and let you know," responded Abuk.

In that instant they both comprehended the reality of what Abuk had just said and together, as in unison, they both sobbed quietly. The thought of their separation was too difficult to bear at this particular moment.

"Perhaps the couple will take you for rides in the snow," Aben said finally.

"That would be nice … and fun."

Again there was a brief silence, finally broken by Aben. "What would you like most there—in Canada, I mean?"

Abuk took some time to think over the question. When the response came it was almost too quiet for Aben to hear.

"Peace."

"What?"

"I want peace, Aben—the kind of peace that we have only dreamed about before. To sit in the snow on a quiet night and have the experience of holding it in my hands. The peace to look at the stars without worrying about if we will be attacked or have to move on again in the morning. The peace to plant a flower and be there long enough to watch it fully grow. The peace to sing and not worry that someone will try to stop me. The peace to … to pray in quietness and not be troubled."

To Aben it was as though she had just heard a beautiful poem, one that made peace so real that it almost seemed possible. And Aben realized, there and then, that there could be no place else for this girl. In truth, Abuk's heart was a quiet castle of strength and solitude. Yet such a heart could never achieve its goal because Sudan was a country at war and that kind of peace was beyond the realm of the possible.

Abuk looked at her then, her eyes full of pain but depth. "And Aben, I want the peace to think about you and Mana without feeling so hurt by it all. I want to think of the two of you as the bravest and kindest women in the world. I will think of what you would be doing if the war ended and the crops were full."

Both gazed into the fire. After what seemed a very long time, Abuk said: "And I want to know that you will be all right, Aben. I need to know that you will survive because I have survived."

It was all too much for the woman. She scooped Abuk up with surprising strength and held her to her breast. "This I promise you," she said firmly. "I will survive if you do, Abuk. But please, please fight to survive so that we can see one another again." The rest of the night was spent in utter silence and thought.

Hope Fading

Two months later things were not as hopeful as they had been. The Chief had been to see Aben to say that he had received word that the couple from Canada were attempting to negotiate some way of getting Abuk out of the country and back to Canada. But they would not be coming to Sudan until such arrangements were made.

The news did little to improve Abuk's physical condition. Her health had deteriorated to the point where she could no longer keep down solid food; whenever she attempted to eat something substantial, she ended up throwing the food up within minutes. As the problem got worse she began losing significant amounts of weight.

The village worried, and the Chief felt frustrated that he was unable to communicate with the Canadians about the seriousness of the situation. Aben fretted that all her hopes for the girl would come to nothing and that Abuk wouldn't live long enough to fulfill her promised future.

All of this was of little concern to Abuk. She spent her days and nights lying on her cot in a deep fever. Occasionally, in the cool of the evening, Aben would carry her out under the stars and sing to her, but the girl hardly seemed to notice. She appeared remarkably at peace despite her condition.

What no one knew or witnessed was the constant presence of Mana hovering over her child in the privacy of the tukul. Often holding the girl in her arms, Mana sang the songs they sang together years before. Although at times Abuk was hardly conscious, her mother spoke to her of her dreams for the child's future.

Yet it was becoming clear even to Mana that time was running out. She had been sent by God to prepare Abuk for her journey to a faraway place, but on certain days it seemed as though death was only moments away.

Nevertheless, Mana trusted that she wouldn't have been sent if it was all to end in disappointment and death. With hope in her own heart, she encouraged Abuk to struggle on, to keep her strength, and to trust in the future.

The fate of children often becomes more important to adults than their own concerns. This was the state Aben was in. For years she had taken the charge seriously to care for Abuk and provide her the best chance for survival. She had given everything to the effort and though, at times, she found it almost overwhelming, she had dedicated herself to the welfare of the child.

It was this very commitment and concern that contributed to Aben's sense of guilt. In her heart she felt as if she had failed in her responsibility and even the Chief's encouraging words couldn't remove the feeling.

Lost in such thoughts, Aben, knowing that Abuk was sleeping, ventured outside of the village in search of more firewood. Whatever twigs she found she placed on a bare patch of earth and then went off looking for more.

Returning with a few of the small branches she found, Aben was shocked to see the pile of wood much bigger than she had remembered. What has happened here? she asked herself, just as the lone figure of a woman came through some brush carrying a large supply of wood.

"This is my pile," Aben asserted.

The woman lifted her face to Aben and said quietly, "The war has stripped us of everything, even the means to have a fire, but there is always room for friendship among our people. I saw you searching and I thought you could use some help."

"Thank you," Aben said quietly. "I know you. I've seen you before," she continued. And then she remembered the kind woman who had sat with her by the fire when she considered whether to let Abuk go to Canada.

"I haven't seen you for … for," …

"More than two months," the woman said. "And it has been a hard two months. Our land is becoming more and more desolate as this war continues. Surely it can't continue like this."

"Too many have died," Aben said.

"And are dying," the woman responded quickly.

She has done it again, Aben thought to herself. In a similar way as their last meeting, this special woman appeared to know what Aben was facing.

"I have heard of Abuk's situation and it must be hard to wait for the foreigners," the woman said quietly.

"It is too hard," Aben blurted. "There is not enough time left."

"Time is in God's hands, Aben—you have known that better than anyone. Goodness and grace come as they are required."

Aben flashed out in anger. "They have been required for months now but nothing happens."

The woman gently took Aben's hand in her own and was quiet for some time.

"The girl will survive as long as we don't lose our own personal hope," she said finally. "Abuk is fighting her own battles, but you have your own. It is now time for you to face them directly."

Aben stuttered out a reply: "How ... face what?"

"You have made the same mistake as so many of our people. As loved ones have perished, some of our hope went with them. Enough of them die and we suddenly find we have nothing left. What will we have then to rebuild our country when peace finally comes? Will the women of Sudan be barren shells, incapable of hoping and trusting, or will they teach our children and show our men of a future blessed by God?"

"But there is little else for us but a bleak future," Aben responded heatedly.

"Millions of us yet live, Aben, and peace is nearer than you think. Your skills will be required for this village to move ahead. The Chief can do only so much. It will be you and your leadership that can guide this place to a new day. Do not make the mistake of linking your hope exclusively with Abuk's. Her future is secure—you must now move on with yours!"

Aben was speechless, not knowing what to say. The kind of passionate speaking she had just heard reminded her of the courage of her mother who had lived during Sudan's most difficult years. The truth was that she wanted to believe the woman's words and it was that small belief that lit a spark of hope in her spirit. However, she was not quite ready to admit it.

"Perhaps there comes a time when the opportunity for peace has passed. I used to feel its pull on my heart, but it has gone."

"Oh, Aben, I don't think so," responded the woman kindly. "You are not to be underestimated and I refuse to do so. Can you not feel it now, Aben? Do you not sense within our people a glimmer of hope that peace is coming? Leaders are meeting with our opponents right now, attempting to resolve their differences. Have you not sensed the bombings decreasing? There are not as many raids of our villages—have you not noticed it?"

Truthfully, Aben hadn't, and she now understood why. She had joined her spirit to Abuk's and as the child was failing so was her own hope for the future. She considered what she had just heard and realized that the war had lessened somewhat. She recalled certain singing in the village as the people heard news of the peace talks, yet the joy had never struck her because she was too busy thinking of Abuk. She and Abuk had been in the same village now for almost three months—something that would never have happened a year ago. She recalled how they had to move on every few days to escape capture. But this was no longer the case. How had she not seen that?

She turned to face the woman, a smile lightly crossing her face. "Abuk is such a wonderful child that her personality captures all who know her. I have been a willing captive, though she never asked it. You are right. Her world has become mine and her dying has become mine."

"She is not dying," the woman said.

"And neither am I," Aben said firmly. "I have seen you three times in the last few months and on each occasion you have given me a timely word, something to help me face the future. One time you reminded me that the women of south Sudan are destined to suffer for their loved ones, but this time you revealed to me the other side, the side that points to our ability to overcome anything we face. And, oh, what we have faced," Aben said with a chuckle. "Will anyone ever know how we have suffered?" she asked.

"They will if we live to tell the tale, Aben."

Hours later Aben would recall the woman's wise words. Gazing down at Abuk's sleeping form she realized that things had quietly become different for her. *This child must live* she thought to herself and in her heart she committed herself once again to the child's survival.

But there was something more, something noble. She now understood that whatever happened to the child, the people of south

Sudan had to go on and she had an important role to play in that journey.

Gently, she lowered herself beside the sleeping Abuk and placed her arms around the child. Abuk murmured slightly but didn't awake. And for the first time in many months Aben slept with a spark of hope shining in her heart.

From Afar

Over the next few weeks Abuk's condition would worsen and then, just as suddenly, improve somewhat. Yet all in the village knew she couldn't live in such a state much longer. The Chief attempted to find a way to take her a great distance away to a medical clinic run by a non-governmental organization, but it was clearly too far—the child wouldn't have survived the journey.

For her part, Abuk seemed to realize that she had little time left. And instead of making her sad, she somehow accepted it. No one knew or understood that Mana had been speaking to the child constantly, encouraging her to stay strong. That strength made people think Abuk simply didn't care, when in reality she was doing her best to survive, as her mother had taught her.

And then one morning, not too long before noon, the distant drone of an airplane engine could be heard. Such sounds were common to the people of south Sudan. Sometimes the planes brought food but other times they would drop bombs and destruction. Villagers had come to learn the different sounds of the engines and on this particular morning they knew it was a friendly plane, probably bringing supplies.

Suddenly the plane swooped overhead, arousing Abuk from her slumber. She listened as best she could and realized it was heading for the airstrip in Malualkon, some five kilometres away. She never thought anything more of it and drifted back to sleep.

As they had on other occasions, villagers slowly began the walk to the airstrip to see if they could secure any supplies for their families or the sick, like Abuk. Aben wanted to go with them but knew she shouldn't leave Abuk alone.

People were nervous. Fighting had erupted in the closest village to Yargot and everyone wondered if the enemy forces were advancing in their direction. It was as it had ever been—hope for resources and fear of war.

Aben was busy fixing the thatched roof of the tukul which the termites had partially destroyed. She quickly faced north as she heard the distant *thwump* of a deadly shell exploding. What should she do? She had no way of knowing if the fighting was advancing in her direction, but if it was she would need to get Abuk out as quickly as possible. She forgot all about the roof and began the process of packing up what belongings would be essential if they needed to leave the area quickly.

After a full hour Aben determined that the violence was indeed coming closer, though quite slowly. "Abuk, Abuk, it's time to wake up. We need to travel."

The child opened her eyes and murmured something but showed no sign of activity.

"Come, come, we must get moving."

Aben attempted to lift Abuk off the cot but the child's body was limp. The woman was just in the process of pulling Abuk up when she heard the sound of an automobile engine. For a brief moment it sent a shiver of fear into her heart because she thought it might be a vehicle full of enemy soldiers. Abuk, too, opened her fearful eyes, as if she was having the same thoughts.

"Sshhh," Aben whispered, placing her finger over her lips. She knew there was no use in running now—Abuk would never make it. Aben sat down on the floor next to Abuk and prayed as she had never prayed before. "God, not now, not like this. Let this child live," she pleaded through her tears.

And then she heard footsteps, many of them. Protectively she placed her arm around Abuk and listened closely. A smile crept on her face as she recognized the voice of the Chief. But he was speaking a different language. And a moment later she heard a woman's voice, speaking a similar tongue and she grew fully confused.

"Aben ... Aben, are you in there? It is safe—come out." The Chief's words were positive and Aben detected a note of excitement in his tone. She left Abuk on her cot, stood up, and made her way outside. What she saw next stunned her.

"What took them so long?" Aben asked a few minutes later.

The Chief took his time before answering. "They had been told Abuk was in another village west of here. They only came to Malualkon as a last resort, hoping she would be there."

Aben looked at the Canadian couple, with their whitened skin and perplexed smiles. Strangely, at least in her mind, they didn't appear at all nervous. In fact the woman even knew some words of Dinka. Then she recalled what the Chief had told her days before: they had been to south Sudan many times. Interestingly, that thought put her at ease. They must be committed to our people to come so often, she thought to herself.

The Chief said something in the English tongue to the couple and they slowly moved forward. Acting as an interpreter, he introduced the two strangers to Aben. She shook their hands respectfully and was delighted when the woman said *chebak*, the native Dinka greeting.

Quickly Aben recalled the explosions from earlier. "This is not safe for them," she said to the Chief. "Do they not know of the fighting?"

To her surprise the Chief nodded his head, adding, "They were told at their last stop but they wanted to come anyway."

Aben gave them a grudging smile of respect, but noticed the woman looking curiously at the entrance to the tukul. It was then that Aben heard Abuk moaning and she instinctively understood that the Canadian was being drawn into Abuk's world.

And then, suddenly, another explosion was heard, not close, but loud enough to make everyone talk at once. At that moment the soldiers accompanying the Chief began signalling that everyone should leave quickly. As they moved toward the woman to take her back to the truck, the woman's husband put himself between them and his wife with a resolute look on his face. Not sure what to do, they looked at the Chief.

"We must go soon," he said to his visitors.

It was as though the woman hadn't heard him. "May I?" she asked respectfully. When no one moved, Aben leaned forward and pulled the curtain back from the opening.

Within a minute everyone was crowded into the dark confines of the tukul. The woman inched forward to the cot and knelt beside Abuk. Gently, she touched the child's forehead and felt her high temperature.

For all the others it was as if the moment had become sacred. No one dared speak or move. They watched in fascination as Abuk opened her eyes and looked directly at her visitor. In her ear she heard a familiar voice: "This is the one, my daughter. This is the couple. It is time."

To the shock of everyone, Abuk took the woman's hand, attempting to rise. It was something no one had expected. She understands, Aben thought to herself. God be praised, she understands.

"I think it's time to leave," said the Canadian man, his voice reminding people of the urgency. The Chief quickly gave out some commands and the group helped in lifting Abuk and moving her towards the waiting truck.

Lost in it all was Aben. She watched the party moving towards the vehicle and was totally overcome with emotion. And then as they placed Abuk in the woman's arms in the back of the truck, the visitor raised her arm and motioned for Aben to be seated beside her. "Is that all right?" she asked the Chief.

"It is natural," he replied with respect.

Unsure what to do, Aben just stood there. The male visitor quickly jumped down from the truck, walked to her, and gently took her arm. Hesitant at first, Aben allowed herself to be guided by him to the edge of the truck, where some of the soldiers lifted Aben aboard. A spare tire rested on its side just behind the cab and the visitor was seated on it. The woman once again called on Aben to sit next to her. And when she finally seated herself, she was overcome when the woman lifted the child onto Aben's lap. It was an act of kindness, respect and friendship that Aben was never to forget.

Quickly the truck was put in gear and began driving through the trees. Everyone laughed when a soldier raised his hands into the air and broke out in a song of Sudan. For the first time in the memory of anyone there, someone had come to their own village to take a child to a place of freedom in another country. The soldiers rejoiced at a mission accomplished. And the two women joined their hearts in a spirit of shared responsibility and a sense of hope.

Abuk opened her eyes and looked up directly into the gaze of the woman. She saw nothing but love and gentleness. *Mana, you were right ... she is like us.* And then she shut her eyes in pain as she thought she would be leaving her village for the last time. Worse still, she would never see her mother again.

Planning the Future

For three hours the truck drove, often journeying through other villages where people came out to see the strange sight of two white-skinned people and a truck full of soldiers. Abuk slept for most of the trip while the Canadian couple and Aben sat silently. The soldiers, however, continued singing and bringing smiles to the faces of everyone in the vehicle.

At last they came to a Roman Catholic Mission which housed a school and some primitive medical facilities.

As they began to exit the truck they noticed a short man in a priest's robe walking towards them. He and the Chief shook hands and obviously knew one another.

"Ah, here are our Canadian friends," the priest said in very good English. "I am Father Thomas Oliha, and I direct the mission here. We invite you to stay with us if you can."

His smile was so bright and happy that the couple gladly accepted his invitation. Wearily they got out of the truck, with Aben carrying Abuk. "So this is the child," the priest said quietly. "I didn't think you would find her."

"This couple has been very persistent," the Chief said in Dinka, leaving the couple to wonder what they were saying.

"I heard from some people here that they were heading to your village, but with the fighting going on, it just didn't seem possible,"

Father Thomas said quietly.

"It seems as if today everything is possible," Aben said for the first time. Everyone nodded in agreement as they moved towards the buildings of the mission compound.

"Father Thomas," the Canadian woman said as she touched his elbow. "This child is very sick. Is there anyone here who can assist her?"

The sadness on the priest's face provided the answer before he even spoke. "We have a clinic here, but no doctors and few supplies. Nevertheless we have someone who knows a bit about medicine. Give the child to me and I'll take her there right away."

Following behind him, the party made its way to a cement block building that looked fairly new. Though it was supposed to be a small medical clinic, its rooms were dark and empty.

"Let's leave Abuk here for now while we get you settled in your rooms," the priest said. Reluctantly they took a final look at the sick child before following him. In everyone's mind it seemed as though there wasn't much time left for Abuk and that thought filled them with a sense of deep sadness.

Two hours later they all met in the meal room, where the Catholic sisters had prepared a special meal of potatoes, goat and warm, freshly-made buns.

Even though he tried to make everyone comfortable, it was clear to Father Thomas that the Canadian couple was troubled by the child's health. "She is not as you expected?" he asked quietly.

"Actually, I have worried for days now that she might have died. The fact she is still alive is a blessing to us." The Canadian woman's words were strangely comforting to the priest.

The door opened and in walked the young man who was responsible for looking at Abuk's physical condition. "Without having the proper facilities I can't be sure, but I think the child has pneumonia in both lungs and she is filled with parasites. That's why she has not been able to put on any weight in the last year. There is also a good chance that she has tuberculosis, and that is serious indeed."

It was what they all had expected, but still the news was devastating. "The best thing is to get her to a proper hospital, preferably in Kenya."

"I have radioed for a plane to come to the airstrip here in two days time," the priest said. "Will she be all right until then?"

"Given the circumstances, this is probably the best place she could be right now," the young man answered.

Later they all sat drinking tea, pondering what to do next. Finally the man from Canada asked, "It is important for us to know if Abuk has any family before we even begin the process of adopting her. Can you help us with this?"

All eyes travelled to Aben and the Chief. "The child's mother was from our village and I knew her before she was taken away in captivity to the north. She had a sister that was taken away at the same time, but as far as I know there was no one else. People lost contact with the sister years ago and it's doubtful she is still alive. If Abuk's mother had any other children in the north we are unaware of it, although we did hear one time that there had been a sister and a brother. But we never heard anything more about it - I doubt it is true. I have consulted extensively in the village and we are all of agreement that this is a lone child."

The couple permitted a smile to cross both their faces at this news, for it meant that Abuk could indeed be taken to Canada to be adopted.

The Canadian woman looked at Aben and asked the question that everyone knew would eventually be asked. "You have cared for this child for years now. Neither my husband nor I would feel comfortable taking her away if you wished to keep her."

"The child does not belong to Aben," the Chief interjected suddenly. "She was placed in charge of the child by the village elders and she has fulfilled her role. But she is not the mother."

"And neither am I," the woman answered immediately, causing everyone in the room to look at her. "Aben has done more for this child than I have and yet you are willing to let Abuk come with us. She has earned the right to make this decision."

"Do you agree with this?" the Chief asked the woman's husband.

"Absolutely," was his only reply.

The Chief interpreted for Aben and all was quiet then as they waited for her to answer.

"Our people have always lived and died in this land. Sometimes we don't think that there is a world beyond this place. But in other countries people are free to travel around the world, to pursue education in other places and even find employment in foreign cities. In her short time on this earth, Abuk has had her share of Sudan. Like her mother, I'm sure, I would want her to have an education, the finest kind. This couple and Canada can give her those things and we would be fools to deny them to her."

Aben paused momentarily, thinking of her next words. "But none of that will matter if she doesn't live. Nothing in Sudan can save her now. Her only help is the medical opportunities in places beyond our borders. It is not enough for Abuk to get healthy, she must stay that way, and Canada sounds like just such a place."

The last words were said with tears in her eyes. Everyone in the room understood how hard it was for Aben to say she thought the child should leave, and yet they all knew she was right. Everyone remained deep in thought.

"These are difficult times requiring us to make difficult decisions. But of this we are all in agreement: the welfare of the child is more important than anything else. Hopefully you know we understand this," the Chief said, looking at the visiting couple. "And now, finally meeting you, we can see that Abuk will have new parents that not only care deeply about her, but about her country as well. We are in your debt."

What more could be said after such words? The Chief had only voiced the sentiments that were in the room, but had done so with a quiet dignity and respect.

"And so we have two days to prepare for the child's journey," the Chief said. "For official reasons there should be paperwork completed during that time. We should also have proper medical documents drafted up before you leave. And also, our two visitors should spend as much time with Aben as they can so that they can learn of Abuk's past. Is there anything else?"

"We only need one more thing," the Canadian woman said with an appreciative smile.

"What's that?"

"A celebration."

A Community Gathers

They came from every part of the region, some walking for as many as four days. News had quickly spread of the Canadian visitors and the fate of the child and many came to see for themselves what was actually taking place.

The final night—Saturday—was to be a celebration of new friendship and prayers for the child. The local military commander had offered food for as many as came and by the time darkness descended the mission compound was filled to capacity.

In Sudanese fashion, people moved around and talked for almost two hours before any kind of speech was given. The Canadian woman and Aben sat together on plastic chairs, each taking turns sitting with Abuk in their laps. Abuk herself was aware of all that was happening but she was too weak and tired to do much but observe. In truth she felt despondent at the thought of not seeing Mana again. The time for leaving was near and the closer it came the sadder she became.

After a time Abuk began to feel ill again and Aben took her into the metal hut to rest. "Are you all right?" she asked the child quietly, sensing that something was troubling her.

"I just need some sleep," Abuk responded. Aben left her then and went back out to join the large group. Just as she seated herself in the chair, the Chief rose and began speaking.

"I wish to thank the commander for his generosity tonight because it is a special occasion. Tonight we are made aware that there are people in this world who are concerned for our sufferings in this land. We have always known they existed because of their dropping food and supplies from airplanes. But here in this place we have come face to face with people from Canada who have asked to take one of our own back with them to their country."

A quiet buzz ran through the crowd as some were hearing this news for the first time. Others patiently waited for what the Chief would say next.

"Along with other elders, I have investigated the child's history and we have determined there are no relatives who can provide for the child. And our own village barely has food for the rest of us. Therefore we have granted the request of this couple to adopt the child. They have the approval of their own government and even our own political leaders."

This caused grunts of respect and appreciation from many of those gathered. They had been unaware of how much work had gone into this special adoption.

"Our people have been used to a life of slavery and lack of opportunity. For this one child that is about to change. Our friends have come here, not just to save a child, but to remind us to hope that we might yet see other countries intervening on our behalf. We know of their compassion because long before they came for this child they had been helping our people in other areas of the south for many years. This alone would have convinced our elders to release the child into their care.

"But there was another important factor. Two days ago they informed us that if anyone had an objection to this adoption that they would not proceed with the legalities. This impressed us, for they wished our community to have the final say."

A smattering of applause broke out in the crowd at the hearing of this. As the Chief went on, more and more of them directed their gaze to the Canadian man and woman.

"We are a people of faith," he began again. "Indeed, it is this faith that has sustained us through all these years. And for this reason I have asked our own good Father Thomas to provide his blessing on this unique adoption."

All watched as Father Thomas thanked the Chief and turned to face the crowd directly. Almost immediately he had their attention.

"Brother and sisters, this is a good day for us. This is a day that God has made and we rejoice in it. For one of our own who appeared destined to leave this life early has in fact had her story heard in a faraway country. And we have a couple here who came all this way to make sure this child's life did not end in tragedy, as so many others have during these years of conflict.

"Brother and sisters, I ask you to bless them, as I bless them. For in the adoption of this child they have ceased to become Canadian visitors to us. In fact they have ceased to be Canadian. By becoming the parents of Abuk they have become Dinka, southern Sudanese."

Father Thomas grabbed the hand of the man in one of his own hands, the Canadian woman's in the other, and said with a loud voice: "This is our brother. This is our sister. Our worlds are now one through the life of a special child. As we accept them, so they must accept the culture of this child. They must remind her of her special place in this community, even though she is far, far away. They must remind her she is Dinka, a woman of Sudan, so that in later years this can become a significant source of pride for her. For indeed, she is our representative in a far-off place and we all pray that she will represent her people well. Brothers and sisters, I now present to you our newest community members."

As he held up their hands, all present began to clap and even to sing songs. The priest's blessing now paved the way for the celebrations to truly begin. People surged forward to shake the hands of the couple. One of the Roman Catholic nuns pulled them into a circle and began dancing, urging them to join her. Soon others joined and the night became a time of joy the likes of which the community had not known for many years.

Abuk listened to the songs as they filtered through the night towards her building. She knew the happiness was for her and she wanted to appreciate it more, yet she couldn't. She cried in silence, her sickness only making the moment even more painful.

"It is hard to leave the place you love, the people you have grown to care for."

"Mana … Mana," Abuk cried. "Where are you? I can't see you in the dark."

And then she felt her mother's cheek against her own and strong arms pulled her closer.

"You are worse than the last time we talked," her mother said.

"I know. I know. I have tried, Mana, but my body cannot fight anymore. Please believe me, I have been trying to be brave, as you asked."

The child's pleading words touched her mother's heart. "And you have done it, Abuk—just as I knew you would."

The embrace lasted a long time, as both listened to the happiness outside. "I don't recall our people being this joyful since I was a child, almost the same age as you. It is wonderful. And all of it is for you."

"I understand now, I think," Abuk responded. "You are an angel God sent to prepare me for this moment."

"Abuk, listen to me carefully. I am no angel. I am your mother.

It is true I died, yet God heard my prayers and sent me here to get you ready. You are to have new parents—a mother and a father. You are blessed."

"They will never be you," the girl responded, almost in a whisper.

"They are not meant to be and they know that," Mana said.

The mother felt a slight shudder in the girl's body and pulled her tighter.

"So, it's tomorrow then," Abuk said without looking up.

"It is tomorrow and it will be the start of your future."

"Will you be there … at the airstrip, I mean?"

"Of course. I am your mother, Abuk, and I couldn't be more proud. Just think, my child will live free and go to university. How could I not be there?"

"Tomorrow will come soon," Abuk said, now emotional. "But for tonight will you stay with me, Mana? This one last time?"

Mana pulled herself up beside her daughter and placed her head next to Abuk's. "These hours belong to us—of course I will stay. But tomorrow, Abuk … tomorrow belongs to you."

The young girl had already drifted off to sleep.

Taking Wing

The engine's rumble could be heard even before the plane was spotted. The brilliant sun shining off its wings gave it the appearance of something like a celestial messenger. Instinctively people pulled away from the airstrip in preparation for all the flying dust that would soon fill the air.

Hundreds of southern Sudanese had come to the strip in the morning, waiting in the hot sun for the plane's appearance. The planned arrival time had been delayed and it didn't touch down until early in the afternoon. As it taxied to the end of the airstrip where everyone gathered, the pilot turned off the engines and all suddenly became quiet.

The couple from Canada seemed hesitant about what to do next and chose to let the Chief make the decisions. As the pilot unloaded supplies, the Chief quietly motioned for Aben to bring Abuk forward.

"It is time," he said quietly. And then, with an air of ceremony, he added, "We present this child to you and ask that you bring her up with all the hopes and aspirations of her people here." It was all he said but it filled the moment with importance.

"My friends ... my friends, God go with you and with this blessed child," Father Thomas said loudly. His broad smile was contagious and somewhat eased the sadness many were feeling. "We will pray for this child every day in our parish, but you must also pray for us every day and in this way we will stay a community and encourage one another.

The Canadian woman slid forward and placed her arms around Aben in a manner that caused all to watch silently. "Please tell Aben that we will tell Abuk often of her importance to her life. And also tell her that we will send regular updates by mail, telling her how Abuk is doing."

The Chief translated these words to Aben, who merely nodded silently, attempting to hold back her tears.

Quietly, the Canadian couple moved a bit farther away and left Aben and Abuk alone. "This couple will send me letters, Abuk, so when you can, please write me too and know that I will keep you in my heart always."

Although Abuk felt she had no more tears to shed, her eyes brimmed with tears again. "I will come back ... I give you my word, Aben."

The older woman lifted her chin so that their eyes met. "The only thing that matters now is that you promise me you will live. You will be going to strange places, with people doing tests on you and you will be afraid. But don't give up, child, stay strong so that we might yet meet again."

"We must get them on the plane," said the Chief. Then the man from Canada approached Abuk and held out his two hands. Hesitantly at first, she came forward until their hands met. Then with a quick movement he lifted her into his arms, after which he placed a hand on Aben's shoulder. "Thank you, Aben," were his words in English, but Aben understood.

It was then the Canadian woman's turn to approach Aben. Without a word she embraced Aben and quietly shuddered. For both of them it was a moment of deep pain. In truth, this was the moment of exchange, the final farewell.

As the couple walked towards the plane's steps the crowd began yelling Sudanese chants and waved in happiness. No sooner had they boarded the plane and closed the door then a deep grief flooded Aben.

And then suddenly, in the window, was the Canadian woman's face. With her hand she was waving. Everyone waved back … everyone but Aben. She began running towards the airplane and stood outside the door. Through the window she could see the Canadian woman saying something to the pilot. The door quickly opened and Aben ran up the steps.

For the woman from Canada it was a moment of fear, for she thought Aben had changed her mind and wanted Abuk back. Aben stopped in front of her, touching the woman's cheek. But then she quickly bent down and grabbed Abuk's face. "I love you, child … I love you as my own. You are blessed with so many people to love you, but always remember this place. Remember Sudan, Abuk, and your brave mother."

"And you," Abuk whispered softly.

"And me,"

With that, Aben nodded one more time to the Canadians in farewell and descended the stairs, walking into the crowd.

Moments later the plane began to taxi, getting ready for take off. People on the ground waved madly and called out their goodbyes.

Abuk lifted herself on the man's lap and peered longingly out the window. In desperation now, she looked for the one person she desired to see above all others. And then she spotted Mana, standing beneath a tree farther down the runway.

As the plane sped past, Mana wiped the tears from her eyes as she lifted one hand in goodbye. For the briefest of moments their eyes met and it was too much for the girl. In deep despair she wailed out her mother's name, beating at the window.

The Canadian couple were stunned, unable to know what was happening. They tried to quiet Abuk but all they could hear in Dinka was, "Mana … Mana … I love you,"

"What is she saying?" the man asked his wife.

"I don't know," she answered in sadness. "But whatever it is, we must never let Abuk forget this place and the love of these people."

"And Abuk's mother," the man said.

"Above all, her mother," his wife responded.

Though Abuk continued to scream, the strength of the man's arms was somehow comforting and she drew support from his caring grasp. Slowly her eyes closed.

The plane lifted off at the end of the runway and banked steeply to make one final pass over the people. The pilot wagged the plane's wings and everyone waved back with joy. Aben held her hands up high and offered a prayer of thanks for the child's rescue.

Farther down the airstrip, goats now grazed around the base of the tree where Mana had stood. She was gone.

Epilogue

The truck pulled into the mission and unloaded its passengers in front of the church. Soon people began to gather around the vehicle and its strange passengers.

"How do you feel?"

Abuk looked at her Canadian mother with a sense of mixed emotions. It had now been six years since she had left this place and this was her first visit back. "I feel ... confused," she responded finally.

A strong arm fell around her shoulder and her father's voice whispered, "That's a good thing. It will sort itself out." Appreciating his hug more than his words, Abuk laid her head against his shoulder briefly before turning to see what all the commotion was.

From out of one of the buildings, an aging Catholic priest approached them in white robes and an even whiter smile. "Ah ... at last, at last. Welcome my friends." Father Thomas hugged the couple before finally facing Abuk. "We have waited for this day for six years, Abuk, but I would never have recognized you. You seem so ... strong."

In truth she was. Though she was now fourteen years old, the girl was already taller than her Canadian parents. But what struck Father Thomas the most were the classic lines on her face. "You are a true Sudanese woman," he said in appreciation.

"Come, the nuns have prepared some food for you."

None of the visitors was hungry but they all desired something to drink. The nuns and Father Thomas bustled around the dining room, renewing old acquaintances and marvelling at the change in the girl.

Following lunch the priest felt the need to speak again. "Abuk, your parents have been back here many times but somehow their visits never seemed complete—for them or for us. But now you are here. We are a community once again and God is good."

Abuk understood what he was saying but she still felt strange and a bit nervous.

Suddenly the door opened and in the doorway stood the proud figure of a tall Dinka woman who appeared older than the last time they had seen her.

"Aben," the Canadian woman shouted and immediately rushed into her arms. They had seen Aben a number of times over the last six years and a lasting friendship had been built.

But in this moment Aben's eyes only focused on one person. She and the girl stared at one another momentarily and in that instant it was too much for Abuk. In Canada she could always picture Aben in her mind and in truth she greatly desired to see her again. But right now there was just so much happening, so many conflicting emotions.

Aben held out her hand and Abuk took it hesitantly. And then to everyone's surprise they walked outside, Aben shutting the door behind them. Everyone knew better than to follow.

After a time the two of them sat under a tree, in the shade. "You look even better than I had hoped," Aben said happily. "Your mother and father regularly sent me letters, with pictures, telling me of your schooling and how your health had improved. Every prayer was answered, little one, every prayer."

At those two words "little one" the nervousness fled from Abuk and she rushed into the woman's arms. How many times had she remembered Aben calling her by that name and how many times had she wished to see Aben again to thank her for all she had done?

"I am so happy to see you, Aben, so happy. Have you been well?"

"Everything has changed here, Abuk. The government and the rebels have signed peace accords. Our cattle are fatter—I am fatter. The water runs freely and schools are being built for our people."

"Mom and Dad told me you were elected the first woman elder in the village."

"First woman elder and first woman delegate to the peace talks. It has happened Abuk, peace has finally come and it suits our people very well."

Abuk looked at her lovingly before saying her next words. "In Canada, my Mom told me of all you have done and accomplished. And every time she would say that she knew you would become a leader among Sudan's women."

Aben smiled at Abuk proudly but said nothing. "And how is Canada?" she asked finally.

"Oh Aben, it is truly a wonderful place. My Dad never stops saying it is the world's greatest country and I can see why he says it. It believes in freedom and the beauty of nature and the right of women to vote and the right to access to hospitals and schools and …"

"Wait," said Aben, "you must take a breath."

They both burst out laughing. Abuk grew serious then. "But everyday they tell me of Sudan and its brave people - they have never let me forget it."

"It is as I hoped," Aben replied.

"Aben, how did you possibly survive all those years having to care for me? There was so little food and water—how did you do it?"

Aben thought about it for a minute before saying, "Because I am Sudanese and because I loved you. We Sudanese woman have always been strong, but when we love we cannot be conquered."

They both remained in silence thinking about what Aben had just said. "Perhaps we should go back inside," she said at last.

"No, not right now," Abuk responded. "Tell me more about the women of Sudan."

Later as they went for a walk, Aben journeyed over to a well to get a drink, leaving Abuk by the path. It was then that Abuk noticed a figure seated by a tree—a figure that seemed familiar. Feeling somehow drawn, Abuk walked towards her.

And in an instant it suddenly became clear. "Mana," she cried.

The woman didn't rise but did give Abuk a warm smile. "You have returned," she said happily. To Abuk she didn't look any older than what she remembered.

"And you have returned," said Abuk. "I didn't think I would see you again."

"We must complete the circle, Abuk. I had to see you one more time to tell you how proud I am of you. I have watched you in Canada and I think you are exceptional."

Abuk smiled at this, saying, "I just knew you were watching—at times I could just sense it. And I think that I came to terms with the fact that your home was now in heaven. But I don't know if I would have made it during those difficult days if you had not come to me."

"God knows the right time and the ways of the heart," said Mana.

Abuk looked over at Aben in the distance. "The two of you ... you kept me going."

"Three of us," Mana replied immediately.

"Three ... who?"

"Your Canadian mother," Mana said. "I think everyone could have been lost in despair, but when we heard she was coming for you it made hope possible."

Abuk realized it was all true. "Really, I've had three mothers."

"And you have had them for a reason. You must give your life for others, child. You have lived a unique life already and it must be for a purpose."

"That is what my parents keep telling me and I know they are right."

"Live your life, Abuk. Enjoy your youth and explore it. But, at the end of it all, you must give back to life—it is how the circle is joined."

"Like us," Abuk observed.

"Just like us."

It was while everyone was dancing and laughing in the evening that Abuk finally felt herself again. Immersing herself so quickly into African culture had required some adjustment but she felt now the blood of Sudan in her own veins. She watched the children and adults of south Sudan as they interacted. *They have survived,* she thought to herself. And now, at last, peace was theirs.

Everyone suddenly burst out laughing and Abuk turned to see her father attempting to dance with one of the nuns. She couldn't count how many times he had made her laugh, but on this occasion she understood something else too: He loves it here. I can see it on his face.

For just a brief moment he looked at her while making a funny face to the crowd, but she could sense in his gaze a depth of love that she never questioned or forgot. She never would.

It was only by accident that she happened to see Aben and her Canadian mother speaking together as friends. To Abuk, her mother had always been someone filled with life and youth and as she watched her now she felt her heart fill with pride.

And then, behind the two women, she saw the form of Mana listening in on their conversation. They didn't know she was there, of course, but that didn't stop her from enjoying the conversation.

As Aben and the Canadian woman broke out into laughter Abuk marvelled to see Mana's eyes flicker in delight. At that very moment her Africa mother looked directly into her daughter's eyes. What those eyes said was something Abuk was never to forget.

"The path has ended. The circle has closed, Abuk, the circle has closed."

THE END

Made in the USA
Charleston, SC
02 October 2011